D1053035

IN
SEARCH
OF THE
SOUL

IN
SEARCH
OF THE
SOUL

John
Cottingham

A PHILOSOPHICAL ESSAY

PRINCETON UNIVERSITY PRESS | PRINCETON AND OXFORD

Published by Princeton University Press
41 William Street, Princeton, New Jersey 08540
6 Oxford Street, Woodstock, Oxfordshire OX20 1TR

press.princeton.edu

Library of Congress Control Number: 2019937989
ISBN 978-0-691-17442-6
ISBN (e-book) 978-0-691-19758-6

British Library Cataloguing-in-Publication Data is available

Editorial: Ben Tate and Charlie Allen
Production Editorial: Jenny Wolkowicki
Text design: Leslie Flis
Production: Merli Guerra and Jacqueline Poirier
Publicity: Jodi Price and Amy Stewart
Copyeditor: Maia Vaswani

Jacket design: Matt Avery / Monograph

This book has been composed in Arno Pro

Printed on acid-free paper. ∞

Printed in the United States of America

10 9 8 7 6 5 4 3 2 1

For LWC, FJW, JTW, and HJC

CONTENTS

The notion of the soul has a long and problematic history, but perhaps surprisingly it has a power and resonance that are still very much alive today. As will be shown in the opening chapter, it is liable to occur in many different contexts, in literary and poetical writings, as well as in ordinary speech, when human beings speak about what matters deeply to them. It surfaces when people talk about the powerful human need to find our true "self" or identity; when they wrestle with the task of leading integrated and morally worthwhile lives; when they search for the love and affection that can give meaning to our existence, or the joy that arises from the sense of being at one with another human being, or in harmony with the natural world. So far from being the exclusive concern of theologians or historians of ideas, the concept of the soul, as I shall hope to show, is one that has a claim to be central to our thinking about what it is to be human.

Human life is a formidable challenge, but we are all necessarily engaged in the struggle to fulfil what is best in our nature, to realize our true selves, and thereby find meaning and completion. The picture of "humanity in quest of the soul," as the first chapter's title puts it, seems to me—for many reasons, which I shall be exploring in what follows—a resonant and fruitful way of expressing this idea. Nothing, of course, compels us to use this terminology. Philosophical discourse is seldom if ever a matter of coercive argument, but has more to do with trying to show

how certain frameworks of interpretation are hospitable to coming to terms with existential and moral challenges inherent in our human predicament.

The methodology and style in much of what follows connects with a goal that has increasingly informed my work in recent years—namely, to promote a more "humane" conception of philosophizing. While in no way discarding the technical tools of the professional philosopher such as abstract argumentation and analysis, whose value and importance are unquestionable, this approach is also ready to draw on the full range of resources available to the human mind, including those that depend on literary, artistic, poetic, imaginative, aesthetic, and emotional modes of awareness. Among the attractions of reflecting on the concept of the soul is that one cannot study it for very long without being drawn into contexts where all these varied modes of awareness are crucially important.

Socrates, the founding father of Western philosophical inquiry, described himself as having a special interest in "the care of the soul,"[1] and this is an enterprise that cannot be undertaken on the level of the intellect alone, but which must involve the whole human person. For each of us, the quest for the soul, as we struggle to discern and bring to fruition what is best in our nature, is part of that ancient project "know yourself" (another injunction taken to heart by Socrates). This is an enormously difficult task, perhaps especially for philosophers, who often fall prey to what Nietzsche called the "hypertrophy of the logical faculty,"[2] but I hope this modest volume at least manages to give some sense of how closely the personal and the philosophical aspects of the search are intertwined.

1. Socrates, as reported in Plato's *Apology*, 30b.
2. Nietzsche, *Twilight of the Idols*, Aphorism 4.

The topic of the soul touches on many areas of philosophy. In what follows the reader will find that questions are broached relating to moral philosophy (chapter 1), history of philosophy (chapter 2), philosophy of mind (chapter 3), philosophical psychology (chapter 4), and philosophy of religion (chapter 5). The topic of the soul is one that demands treatment from many different angles, and it is part of my aim, in this as in much of my recent writing, to promote a broad, "synoptic" conception of philosophical inquiry, where one tries to see how different parts of our world view fit together (or clash).

Though all the five chapters of the book were newly conceived for this volume, in some of the sections I have made use of material from my earlier work, which I am grateful for being able to acknowledge here: in chapter 2, "The Question of Ageing" (*Philosophical Papers* 41, no. 3 [November 2012]: 371–96), *On the Meaning of Life* (London: Routledge, 2003), "Cartesian Dualism: Theology, Metaphysics and Science" (in *The Cambridge Companion to Descartes*, ed. J. Cottingham [Cambridge: Cambridge University Press, 1992], 236–57), and "Descartes and the Problem of Consciousness" (in *Consciousness and the Great Philosophers*, ed. S. Leach and J. Tartaglia [London: Routledge, 2016], 63–72); in chapter 3, "Cartesian Ethics: Reason and the Passions" (in *Cartesian Reflections* [Oxford: Oxford University Press, 2008], chapter 12); in chapter 4, "Integrity and Fragmentation" (*Journal of Applied Philosophy* 27, no. 1 [2010]: 2–14); and in chapter 5, "Descartes, Sixth Meditation: The External World, 'Nature' and Human Experience" (in *Descartes's Meditations: Critical Essays*, ed. V. Chappell [Lanham, MD: Rowman and Littlefield, 1997]).

In reflecting on the topics in the book I have incurred numerous debts to those who have taken part in various seminars and conferences and presentations over the years, most recently at the Centre for the Philosophy of Religion at Heythrop College,

London, which sadly closed in 2018. Among the many friends and colleagues from whom I have learned much, special thanks are due to Fred Aquino, Clare Carlisle, Sarah Coakley, Brian Davies, Max de Gaynesford, Stewart Goetz, Philip Goff, Peter Hacker, John Kekes, Michael Lacewing, Simon May, Iain McGilchrist, Thad Metz, Anthony O'Hear, Stephen Priest, John Schellenberg, Roger Scruton, Eleonore Stump, Samantha Vice, and Mark Wynn. I am particularly grateful to Fiona Ellis and David McPherson for their friendship and philosophical insight, and for being kind enough to read the complete typescript and provide invaluable comments. Thanks are due to Dr. Matt Cottingham for helpful discussion of the scientist's perspective. I should also like to thank Ben Tate of Princeton University Press for his encouragement, Maia Vaswani for her thoughtful and efficient copy-editing, James Curtis for his insightful indexing, and two anonymous readers for their most acute and constructive suggestions.

John Cottingham
West Berkshire, England
January 2019

IN
SEARCH
OF THE
SOUL

1

Humanity in Quest of the Soul

WAGNER. Alas, poor slave! See how poverty jests in his
nakedness! I know the villain's out of service, and so
hungry, that I know he would give his soul to the devil for
a shoulder of mutton, though it were blood-raw.

CLOWN. Not so neither: I had need to have it well roasted,
and good sauce to it, if I pay so dear, I can tell you.

—CHRISTOPHER MARLOWE, *DOCTOR FAUSTUS*

The Risk of Loss

In the legend dramatized by Marlowe and later retold by Goethe,
Faust makes a disastrous bargain: he gains a great deal of power
and pleasure but loses everything that truly matters. Anyone who
thinks that the badness of the bargain hinges entirely on whether
there really is an afterlife has failed to grasp much of the deeper
significance of the story. It's perhaps unlikely that a dramatist
today would write a play about selling one's soul, but even though
the word "soul" may be less commonly found than it used to be,
the underlying idea is very far from obsolete. Philip Pullman's
acclaimed fantasy trilogy *His Dark Materials* describes a world
where people have "daemons," which take the form of animals
who closely accompany them everywhere. In childhood,
people's daemons have the ability to change their shapes frequently, becoming, for example, cats or birds or monkeys, but

in adolescence the daemons "settle" into a single shape. The daemon is closely linked to the life and distinctive personality of each character, and even a temporary separation of people from their daemons causes intense distress. In the course of the story, some of the characters fall into the hands of evil experimenters who use a hideous process called "intercision": a silver guillotine is employed to sever permanently the lifelong connection between a person and his or her daemon. The result is a listless, demoralized individual, bereft of energy and will, already well on the way to dying.[1]

It does not take any great leap to understand Pullman's concept of the daemon as a kind of imaginative representation of the soul, or at least as having something in common with what people mean by that difficult term. Losing your daemon is about the worst thing that can happen to you, depriving your life of its distinctive rhythm and its moral centre. No price, one feels, would be sufficient recompense for losing one's daemon, and (as the "intercision" episode implicitly conveys) no scientific or technological project, no matter what benefits it promised, could justify depriving someone of his or her daemon. Pullman's attitude towards religion is ambivalent (he certainly targets its powerful institutional manifestations), but it is not hard to detect religious overtones in his portrayal of the preciousness and vital importance of one's daemon, calling to mind the question posed in the gospels: "What shall it profit a man if he shall gain the whole world and lose his own soul?"[2]

But what does it really mean to lose one's soul? Outside the realm of fantasy fiction, can we today still take seriously the idea

<hr>

1. This is the fate of Tony Makarios in ch. 13 of Pullman's *Northern Lights* (published in the United States as *The Golden Compass*), the first volume of the trilogy.

2. Mark 8:36 (Authorized Version).

of the soul as something we are in danger of losing, or perhaps have already lost? Many of the most influential thinkers of modernity seem to have thought so. T. S. Eliot, that great prophet of the modern age, watched the seething crowds flowing over London Bridge and declared: "I had not thought death had undone so many."[3] The line deliberately echoes Dante's vision of the lost souls in Hell, severed from their earthly bodies, just as Eliot's unfortunate city dwellers seem to be severed from their souls. Herded together, condemned to a repetitive existence that is messy and pointless, "distracted from distraction by distraction,"[4] they seem to lack any moral purpose, as listless and demoralized as Pullman's tragic victims whose daemons have been forcibly sliced off. And yet all this, Eliot implies, is accepted by most people as quite normal: no one seems to have noticed that anything is amiss. A century before Eliot, the philosopher Søren Kierkegaard wrote:

> A person can go on living fairly well, seem to be a human being, be occupied with temporal matters, marry, have children, be honoured and esteemed, yet it may not be detected that in a deeper sense this person lacks a self. . . . The greatest hazard of all, losing one's self, can occur very quietly in the world, as if it were nothing at all. No other loss can occur so quietly; any other loss—an arm, a leg, five dollars, a wife, etc.—is sure to be noticed.[5]

Instead of "soul," Kierkegaard talks of the "self," or sometimes of the "spirit," but he seems to be speaking of much the same momentous threat as the danger of losing one's soul. Those who

---

3. Eliot, "The Waste Land," pt. 1, line 63; cf. Dante, *Inferno*, canto 3, line 57.
4. Eliot, "Burnt Norton," line 101; later incorporated into *Four Quartets*.
5. Kierkegaard, *Sickness unto Death*, 32–33.

"mortgage themselves to the world," he says, may achieve all kinds of temporal success, but "spiritually speaking they do not exist—they have no self."[6] Even though it can happen imperceptibly, without anyone noticing, the loss of the self is, for Kierkegaard, a catastrophic moral collapse and amounts to nothing less than "sickness unto death." Putting this in theistic terms, Kierkegaard says that in losing my self I am losing that which makes me conscious of "existing before God."[7] The remark comes in Kierkegaard's *Sickness unto Death*, the title of which recalls the gospel story of Lazarus, whose sickness was indeed fatal and who had to be summoned back from the tomb by Christ.[8] Kierkegaard's implicit suggestion seems to be that the plight of one who has lost his or her very self is even graver than this, unless redeemed by renewed consciousness of God.

Though these reflections of Kierkegaard have a strongly theistic, and indeed Christian, stamp, the idea of the self or soul as the precious and fragile moral core of one's being, something that can be irretrievably lost, does not have to be expressed in explicitly religious, let alone Christian, terms. Several centuries before Christ, Socrates reproached his Athenian accusers for being overly concerned with things like money and reputation, but not having the faintest concern for the virtuous conduct of their lives, or the improvement of the most precious part of themselves—their souls.[9] And in some of the later Hellenistic philosophers, the terms "care of the soul" and "care of the self"

---

6. Kierkegaard, *Sickness unto Death*, 35.

7. Kierkegaard, *Sickness unto Death*, 79. See further Carlisle, *Kierkegaard's Fear and Trembling*, 143–44.

8. See John 11:4.

9. Plato, *Apology*, 29d5–e3; cf. 30a6–b1, 31b, 36c.

are closely linked.[10] By the time of the Christian gospels, this linkage is well established, so that the saying quoted earlier from Mark's gospel ("What doth it profit a man if he shall gain the whole world and lose his soul?") appears in Luke as "What shall it profit a man if he gains the world and loses *himself*?"[11]

Lives, we know, can go well or badly. People can be more or less successful, more or less lucky, and advantaged or disadvantaged in many different ways, by birth or geography, or economic circumstances, or physical health. And sometimes such external circumstances can crush someone so completely that no worthwhile human capacities can unfold. But for those able to enjoy at least a basic modicum of health and physical security, there will always be, beyond questions about fortune or misfortune, wealth or poverty, a further more fundamental question about the moral core of their being—the "soul" or self that defines each individual. Have they found themselves, are they at peace with themselves, or have they wasted their lives, pursuing illusory goods at the cost of losing their very souls?

These brief opening remarks have ranged from the fourth century BC through to the time of Christ, and on down to the nineteenth and twentieth centuries and beyond, and it may seem to be moving much too swiftly to assume that ideas from such disparate historical periods can be grouped together. But the essentials of the human condition have not significantly altered in what is, on an evolutionary timescale, the tiniest blink of an eye. Indeed, however often we are told that this or that technical

10. For "care of the soul" (*epimeleia tēs psychēs*) and "care of the self" (*epimeleia heautou*) in ancient philosophy, see Long and Sedley, *Hellenistic Philosophers*, 25C; see also Seneca, *Epistulae morales*, x. For more on these writers, see Hadot, *Philosophy*.

11. Luke 9:24–25.

or scientific development has "altered human life beyond recognition," the existential predicament that confronts human beings is fundamentally the same as it has always been:

> The troubles of our proud and angry dust
> Are from eternity, and shall not fail.[12]

To be sure, these "troubles" may manifest themselves under various guises—as threats to our psychological equilibrium and identity (Pullman), as spiritual and existential anguish (Kierkegaard), as the risk of neglecting the most precious part of ourselves (Socrates). But there is a common thread, insofar as the task of finding or recovering that vital part of ourselves that has been called the "soul" is a task that transcends any given historical circumstance and is inseparable from the human condition. Beyond the imperatives of securing the wherewithal to keep ourselves alive and physically secure, to be human is to be subject to a deeper demand, the requirement to seek, and to find, our true identity. This will not be a merely factual task, like determining our genetic profile; it will involve measuring what we have so far made of our lives against what they are capable of becoming. The demand is inescapable, no matter how much we may try to stop our ears to it. And in the way we finally respond to it we will either find ourselves or lose ourselves.

Dimensions of Soul

It should already be apparent that the notion of a "soul" is an elusive one, and that questions about "finding the soul" may be understood in a number of ways, including the existential, the psychological, the spiritual, the religious, and the moral. In

---

12. Housman, *Last Poems*, no. 9.

the chapters that follow, we shall hope to explore some of these dimensions, though it may not be feasible or desirable to fully separate them or disentangle them. Such separating—such "analysis" or breaking down—can often be of great value in philosophy if we are to have some kind of conceptual map of the terrain to be crossed, but it is arguable that those distinctive and crucially important characteristics of human beings grouped under the label "soul" are best understood synthetically or holistically, as a network of capacities and dispositions that are intimately interrelated and mutually supporting.

This kind of linkage can be seen if we turn to another context in which the term "soul" is commonly employed—a context that at first sight may seem far removed from the grave questions about moral identity and selfhood so far broached. The context in question relates to the spontaneous outpouring of a certain distinctive kind of joyful emotion. In some verses written by the nineteenth-century Irish poet Samuel Ferguson, and often heard set to a traditional Irish folk tune, we find the opening lines:

> Dear thoughts are in my mind,
> and my soul soars enchanted
> As I hear the sweet lark sing
> In the clear air of the day.[13]

As the song develops, it becomes clear that the imagery is an expression of the poet's joy at being accepted by his beloved. But, as so often in poetry, much more is conveyed here than could be captured by a literal paraphrase (and the lyrical power of the verse to suggest more than what is literally asserted is

---

13. Samuel Ferguson (1810–86); a sung version of the poem, performed by Cara Dillon, may be heard at Alberto Ablanedo, "Cara Dillon—The Lark in the Clear Air," YouTube, 29 October 2006, https://www.youtube.com/watch?v=uLoBEC5mNYI.

immeasurably enhanced when it is set to music). It is not just
that the protagonist feels very pleased about what has hap-
pened. The idea of the soul soaring upwards like the lark in the
"clear air" expresses a peculiar upwelling of joyful exaltation,
and it is important for conveying this meaning that the term
soul is employed. For what is suggested by putting it in terms of
soul, as opposed to, say, the mind or the feelings, is that the
event has a spiritual significance for the life of the subject: it
involves his whole sense of self, of who he is, of the meaning of
his existence. Like Othello when he greets Desdemona with the
words "O my Soul's joy!"—the feeling is not merely one of pleasure or delight, but a complete outpouring of spirit:

> It gives me wonder great as my content
> To see you here before me. Oh my soul's joy,
> If after every tempest comes such calm
> Let the winds blow till they have wakened death . . .[14]

Once one starts to reflect on the kind of human experience
referred to here, one realizes that breaking it down into compo-
nent parts—belief, desire, cognition, emotion—would involve
a kind of distortion. Important though the components are, the
use of the term "soul" alerts us to a deeper significance that has
to be understood holistically: the cliché that the whole is greater
than the sum of its parts is here quite true. We are dealing with
something that impinges on the whole person and affects people's
conception of themselves and their lives at many levels of significance, not all of them perhaps accessed by the conscious mind.
In Othello's joy, there is a wonder at having earned the love and
devotion of his spouse, an elation and sense of completion at
being reunited with her, the sense of calm after the tempest of

---

14. Shakespeare, *Othello* [*c.* 1604], act 2, scene 1.

separation, but also a fragile sense of foreboding, a fear that the joy cannot last:

> If it were now to die,
> 'Twere now to be most happy; for I fear
> My soul hath her content so absolute
> That not another comfort like to this
> Succeeds in unknown fate.[15]

For a modern audience watching the play, the vulnerability is made more poignant by the familiarity most of them will already have with the story, and the knowledge of the tragedy that will unfold by the end. The peculiar resonance of Shakespeare's lines here seems somehow linked to a wider sense of the significance of love in human life—how it can give meaning and purpose to someone's existence, and how the yearning that it engenders is bound up with awareness of love's precariousness, and the ever-present risk of loss.

All this is bound up with love's having a *spiritual* significance, a significance that goes far beyond the biological imperatives of reproduction or the urge for sensual or emotional gratification. The yearning for love, and the "soul's joy" that it brings when requited, are connected with the longing for "ontological root-edness," for that which will ground and validate our existence, and give us a sense of being at home in the world, instead of alienated from it and alone.[16] Whether human love can in fact bear the whole weight of being a repository for this kind of long-ing is an open question; and in any case one could no doubt point to perfectly straightforward and genuine cases of attrac-tion and affection that occur without any of these existential

---

15. Shakespeare, *Othello*, act 2, scene 1.
16. See May, *Love: A History*, 7.

undercurrents necessarily rising to the surface. But what is nevertheless conveyed by the idea of love having spiritual significance, or as involving someone's "soul," is that what is at stake has deep importance for the entire life of the individual. To revert to Ferguson's poem, the elation described, which is likened to the lark singing in the clear air, seems to allow the soul to "soar enchanted" precisely because it is no longer just a "feeling," or a psychological "episode," or an "emotional experience" (though it is all these things), but something that has the power to lift us above the world of ordinary mundane existence, something of transcendent importance that seems to make us fully alive to who we are and to the reality we inhabit.

It is worth reflecting for a moment here on the way this upward movement of the soul is described—"my soul soars *enchanted.*" One often hears that modern, secularized Western society has become "disenchanted," meaning in part that our scientific and technological progress has come at the cost of our losing a sense of the sacredness and mystery of things. We may have greater control over the circumstances of our lives, but the world we inhabit has become lifeless, mechanical, an instrument to be used rather than a living presence shot through with beauty and meaning. Although this notion of "disenchantment" is associated with the twentieth-century sociologist Max Weber,[17] there is something more universal in the thought that human beings can easily become bogged down by the drab practical and instrumental demands of day-to-day existence so that life becomes flat and meaningless. But in moments of great emotional power, when the soul "soars," life suddenly becomes re-enchanted.

---

17. The German term is *Entzauberung:* "The fate of our times is characterized by rationalization and intellectualization and, above all, by the disenchantment of the world"— Weber, "Science as a Profession," 20.

A great prophet of the transcendent power of certain emotions and their ability to lift us out of the mundane was the poet William Wordsworth. His "Lines Composed a Few Miles above Tintern Abbey" perhaps have something in common with Ferguson's description of the soaring of the soul, insofar as strong love and affection for a particular person play a prominent role in the poem; but intermingled with that, and forming the specific focus of the exaltation he describes, is a deep love for the beauties of the natural world.[18] When our senses and our imagination are animated with this love, Wordsworth suggests, we are able to experience intense, epiphanic moments when the exaltation rises to such a pitch that "we are laid asleep in body, and become a living soul." In such moments of transcendence,

> the heavy and the weary weight
> Of all this unintelligible world
> Is lightened—that serene and blessed mood
> In which the affections gently lead us on,
> Until . . . made quiet by the power
> Of harmony, and the deep power of joy,
> We see into the life of things.[19]

The message, a recurring theme in so much of Wordsworth's writing, is how communion with nature and our harmonious responsiveness to the living world around can lift us up in joy and serenity; and it is this that leads Wordsworth to describe nature as "the anchor of my purest thoughts," the "guide and guardian of my heart, and *soul* of all my moral being."[20] Here once again we can see the use of the term "soul" signalling that what is

---

18. Wordsworth, "Tintern Abbey."
19. Wordsworth, "Tintern Abbey," lines 40–49.
20. Wordsworth, "Tintern Abbey," lines 110–12, emphasis added.

involved is something of profound significance for the meaning and value of human life. This is one reason why the term "soul" is so valuable, and why the term "self," although as we have seen it has often been used interchangeably with "soul," does not always serve as well. For not all conceptions of the self necessarily carry these strong ethical and evaluative connotations; the self might, for instance, simply indicate an individual's psychological profile or personality, whereas the use of the term "soul" very often points us not just towards the selves that we are, but towards the better selves we ought to be.

This kind of resonance is by no means confined to the world of poetry or the era of Romantic literature. To come closer to our own time, Leon Kass has argued, in a richly evocative study called *The Hungry Soul*, that all our human activities, even seemingly mundane ones like gathering around a table to eat, can play their part in the overall "perfecting of our nature."[21] More recently still, a book published by the ecologically minded architect Christopher Day at the turn of the twenty-first century is entitled *Places of the Soul*. The choice of title points to the need for humans to live, and to design and build their dwellings, in ways that harmonize with the shapes and rhythms of the natural world, and thereby provide nourishment for their deepest needs and longings. As with Wordsworth, this is not just a matter of "aesthetics," but of profound moral and spiritual significance. Day goes on to argue that in place of what is found in so much modern architecture, the "faceless, mineral objects . . . that dominate and sterilize the streetscape at their feet," thus alienating us from our humanity, we need to create "buildings and places of life-renewing, soul-nurturing, spirit-strengthening qualities":

21. Kass, *Hungry Soul*, 227.

If this plea is not taken seriously, we will be known as the generation of destroyers—destroyers of places, of ecological stability and the human in human beings. If it is, we can start to build an architecture of healing, to build places of the soul.[22]

The underlying message is that human beings need to shake themselves free from exploitative and alienating modes of existence and learn to live in harmony with one another and the natural world; and there is a clear connection here with the task of "finding the soul" that we have set ourselves to undertake, or at any rate to understand better. As with some of our earlier examples, the use of the term "soul" need not necessarily involve any explicitly religious ideas—indeed, Day speaks not of the divine or the transcendent, but of recovering the "*human* in human beings." But it is important to see that the term "human" here cannot just be a descriptive one—for clearly, and sadly, constructing sterile tower blocks is just as much a human activity, it is just as much something that we humans do, as a matter of fact, do, as building homes that harmonize with the surrounding land. By calling the dwellings he advocates "places of the soul," Day is referring not just to what human beings *are*, but to what they *should be*. His vision is a not simply a descriptive one, but what philosophers have come to call a *normative* one. So by building for the soul, we are building in a way that transcends what is mean and ugly and utilitarian in our nature, and allows what is best in our human nature to flourish. Like Othello when he greets his "soul's joy," like Ferguson's soul "soaring enchanted" as it yearns for the beloved, like Wordsworth's exaltation of the spirit as he responds to the quietness and beauty of the natural world, what is conveyed by talk of the

22. Day, *Places of the Soul*, 270–72.

"soul" is the aspiration to live up to what is finest in our nature, so that we can be redeemed from the squalor and waste of our quotidian existence, and begin to find healing and completion.

The Soul and Human Nature

In the many and various contexts introduced so far, we have seen the term "soul" being invoked by a number of different writers not in some technical philosophical sense, but in ways that are likely to resonate with large numbers of people, insofar as they highlight certain widely shared and centrally important features of human experience. These include, for example, our anxieties about finding our true "self" or identity; our search to lead integrated and morally worthwhile lives; our yearning for the love and affection that can give meaning to our existence; and the exaltation that arises from the sense of being in loving union with another human being, or in harmony with the natural world.

At this point, however, one may perhaps begin to wonder if the net has not been cast too widely. Are not the various contexts in which we find the term "soul" cropping up simply too divergent and heterogeneous to allow us to suppose the notion of "finding the soul" refers to one single problem or interlinked set of problems?

Part of what is at issue here, when we group together human activities and emotions that are said to involve the soul, is a philosophical problem about human nature. To speak of the importance of the soul, or of a "spiritual" dimension to our experience, implies, at a minimum, that our human lives cannot be fulfilled through mere material or utilitarian gratification, but that our nature demands more. In seeking nourishment for the human soul, we seem to be implicitly presupposing that human nature, despite all its flaws, is somehow oriented towards some higher goal or end than satisfying our biological and social needs as a species. We seem, at least on one interpretation of what is going on here, to be reaching towards some kind of objective pattern or template that determines what it is for human beings to realize what is best and finest in their nature.

But is there such a pattern? A dominant strand in our contemporary secular culture is highly sceptical about this, and regards any such notion as having ceased to be tenable in the light of post-Darwinian understandings of the human species. On this view, human beings are simply a "ragbag," as it were, of genetically determined and culturally inherited propensities and dispositions, with no reason to think there is one right way of living that will suit everyone. Here is Bernard Williams, one of the most eloquent spokespersons for this contemporary view:

> [The] most plausible stories now available about [human] evolution, including its very recent date and also certain considerations about the physical characteristics of the species, suggest that human beings are *to some degree a mess*, and that the rapid and immense development of symbolic and cultural capacities has left humans as beings for which no form of life is likely to prove entirely satisfactory, either individually or socially.[23]

Those attracted to this pessimistic—or, as its advocates would say, realistic—view of human beings will find plenty to object to in the implications of the phrase "finding the soul," if this is taken to mean the goal is to recover a way of living that represents our true human identity—how we are meant to be. For the plain fact, according to Williams and those who share his

23. Williams, *Making Sense of Humanity*, 109, emphasis added.

perspective, is that there is no such identity: instead, there are many and various projects and goals that a human being may adopt, with no reason to think they will all "fit together into one harmonious whole."[24] Or as the American philosopher George Harris puts it, in even starker terms: "Our values are pursued in a world that is very unfriendly and hostile to our efforts and . . . our own deepest values war against each other with tragic results."[25]

There is clearly some truth in this view. No one could deny that human life is often complicated and sometimes tragic. Humans are conflicted beings. And even leaving aside the deeper psychological conflicts, the ordinary task of mapping out one's life obviously involves the need to choose between different and incompatible pathways—one cannot be a farmer and also a sailor, or an academic and also an airline pilot. So much may readily be granted. The question that remains, however, is whether despite all the variations, there is an underlying template for human flourishing, a goal or end towards which all the different pathways should ultimately tend if our nature is to find fulfilment.

Aristotle defined human fulfilment or happiness as an *activity of the soul in accordance with virtue*. What exactly he means by "soul" (*psychē*) will be examined later,[26] but for the present it is enough to note that the soul's activity, for Aristotle, is very much bound up with exercising the various capacities that are characteristic of our species, and that virtue or excellence involves our distinctive human capacity for rationality. We cannot blunder through life relying entirely on instinct or habit. Having formed

---

24. Williams, *Ethics*, ch. 8, 153.
25. Harris, *Reason's Grief*, 15–16.
26. See ch. 2.

the right habits in childhood may be essential for a good life (indeed Aristotle stresses this point), but we also need, he says, to have our life ordered towards a *telos*—a rationally determined end.[27] Once our human capacity for ordered planning and rational evaluation is taken into account, it becomes clear that any worthwhile human life has to be organized so as to provide first the basic prerequisites for a good human existence, such as food and shelter, and then a whole range of personally and socially enriching goods such as family relationships, friendships, and recreational and cultural activities. Furthermore, these will in turn require institutional structures of social cooperation and rational deliberation that enable these goods to develop and flourish. So despite the "messiness" of our human nature, it seems plausible to think rational reflection will enable us to construct a stable list of virtues necessary for the good life that is valid across many different types of situation. The underlying idea here is that our human nature as rational and as social animals requires, if we are to flourish, that our activities, practices, and social systems be rationally ordered towards an end, or *telos*, that represents the good for humankind. In short, as has been argued in our own time by Alasdair MacIntyre, one of the most systematic defenders of this kind of Aristotelian approach, human agents, "as participants in the form of life that is distinctively human . . . can only be understood, they can only understand themselves, *teleologically*."[28]

But is it possible, after Darwin, to believe in this kind of objective, teleological framework in terms of which our lives can find harmony, meaning, and value? To be sure, human beings do aim for various goals, and they work and plan towards achieving

27. Aristotle, *Eudemian Ethics*, bk. 1, 1214b6–14.

28. MacIntyre, *Ethics in the Conflicts*, 223–37, emphasis added.

those goals—there is nothing in evolutionary science that should make us doubt this basic common-sense truth. But why should there be a harmonious rational pattern that subsumes the disparate aims of different individuals? The goal for Don Giovanni was self-gratification and sensual enjoyment; the goal proposed by Nietzsche was power and creativity; the goal of Gauguin was artistic achievement. All these characters might be said to be seeking to realize their unique individual selfhood, and to find a certain kind of exaltation of "soul." So why should we go along with the Aristotelian idea of "*the* good for humankind" (*to anthrōpinon agathon*),[29] or his associated idea of a blueprint for human fulfilment involving virtuous activity of the soul? What justifies the claim to objectivity?

The Soul and Moral Integration

One kind of religious answer to the question just raised would invoke a highly metaphysical account of the soul. The idea here would be that in addition to our biological nature, our collection of often conflicted and mutually warring impulses derived from our mixed cultural and genetic inheritance, each human being has an immortal soul specially created by God, and that our fulfilment can be assured only when the soul is oriented towards the end ordained by our creator. This is Saint Augustine's vision of the restless longing of the human soul that can find repose in God alone.[30] Many have found this an inspiring vision, but interpreting it is not without problems: it may seem to take our conception of the soul too far away from the

---

29. Aristotle, *Nicomachean Ethics*, bk. 1, ch. 7, 1098a16.

30. Augustine of Hippo, *Confessions*, bk. 1, ch. 1: "You have made us for yourself, and our heart is restless until it finds rest in you."

ordinary human context (the context that forms the main focus for Aristotle and his followers) and lead us instead into the metaphysical perplexities of a Platonic-style account, where the soul becomes a kind of ethereal other-worldly part of us that does not obviously connect with our biological nature. We shall return to these issues in the next chapter, and in particular the question of whether a religious idea of the soul does in fact necessarily require us to think of it in "Platonic" or other-worldly terms. But what at any rate seems clear for present purposes is that any conception of the soul that is to make sense as a way of understanding the human condition must be capable of being *integrated into the rest of our world view*: it must fit in with, or at least be compatible with, our scientific picture of ourselves and our origins and our personal experience of the human condition and the moral problems of our existence. With this in mind, let us leave the metaphysical idea of an immaterial and immortal soul on one side for the moment, and pursue the argument about teleology, human nature, and human fulfilment from a more philosophically down-to-earth perspective.

Evaluated even from an ordinary human perspective, the lives referred to at the end of the previous section, the life of sensual gratification (Giovanni), the life built around the will to power (Nietzsche), and the life of single-minded artistic creativity (Gauguin), all turn out to be problematic as coherent blueprints for human fulfilment. For all these lives seem to envisage a good that is defined in fundamentally self-oriented terms. Don Giovanni, in Mozart's opera, makes this explicit: his motto is *"mi voglio divertir"* (I want to amuse myself),[31] and sensual diversion

---

31. From the aria "Gia la mensa è preparata," in Mozart's *Don Giovanni* (1787), act II, scene 24; lyrics by Lorenzo da Ponte.

unashamedly takes precedence over the happiness of others.[32] Or again, Nietzsche's "new philosopher," pursuing the grand designs of the will, is explicitly stated to need a "heart turned to bronze," hardened against the "weakness" of compassion for others that might interfere with his projects.[33] And Gauguin (at least as depicted in what has become in the philosophical literature an icon for a certain kind of single-minded pursuit of artistic success) ruthlessly abandons his family in search of the islands in the South Seas where his painting can flourish.[34] Yet there seems to be something unstable about these kinds of compartmentalized vision in which an individual's projects are supposed to bestow meaning in isolation, irrespective of their moral status and how they impinge on others. Given the kinds of creature that we humans are, something vital for our integrity and psychic health is lost if our chosen projects involve walling in our rational awareness and emotional sensibility so that we are no longer open and vulnerable to the needs and demands of others.

If, as these considerations imply, the compartmentalized life is less than fully human, this in turn suggests that in order truly to flourish, our human lives will have to manifest a certain kind of unity. Some have expressed this in terms of *narrativity*: for the fulfilled human being, there is always a *story* to be told about how I became what I now am, how I learn from my past mistakes, and the destination at which I am now aiming.[35] The kind of narrative unity involved here is to be understood not just in terms of formal coherence or consistency, but as the goal of being able to see one's life as a morally integrated whole. Securing the health of

---

32. For more on the moral implications, see Cottingham, "Demandingness."
33. Nietzsche, *Beyond Good and Evil*, secs. 202 and 203.
34. See Williams, "Moral Luck."
35. See Taylor, *Sources of the Self*, pt. 1, ch. 2, sec. 3.

the precious *soul* or *self,* which no amount of fame or wealth or personal success is worth the risk of losing, will on this account involve the various elements of my life being integrated both diachronically, where past, present, and future are systematically linked as a progressive pursuit of the good, and synchronically, where what I do at any given time is done not in egoistic isolation, but in awareness of how its effects necessarily spread outwards to the lives of others, and in responsiveness to the possibility of discussion and dialogue with them about how my life impinges on theirs and vice versa.[36]

Some contemporary philosophers have challenged the idea that a human life should aspire to narrative unity, and have advocated instead the "episodic" or "happy-go-lucky" life.[37] Such advocacy seems open to a swift and devastating rebuttal: lives of this episodic kind are possible only because others who are not leading happy-go-lucky lives are sustaining the stable relationships and institutions that make their easy-come-easy-go attitude possible.[38] The point can be put in Kantian terms: Can I, as Kant put it, rationally conceive of myself as worthy of respect, without recognizing as a matter of reason that "every other rational being conceives his existence on the same rational ground"?[39] Legislating a privilege for oneself which one will not extend to others shows a defective rationality; for to make use of others as a mere means to one's selfish ends, or even just blithely to ignore one's dependence on and interconnection with them, is to cut oneself off from the operation of the rational

36. Cf. MacIntyre: "The good that is our final end constitutes our lives as wholes, as unities"—*Ethics in the Conflicts,* 229.

37. See Strawson, "Against Narrativity."

38. See MacIntyre, *Ethics in the Conflicts,* 242.

39. Kant, *Groundwork,* ch. 2, transl. Hill and Zweig, 229. See Cottingham, *Meaning of Life,* ch. 1, 25–30.

dialogue that defines our humanity. It is striking, in this connection, that we find the advocates of the "episodic" life tend to be drawn in the end to abandon the very idea of a self persisting over time. Existence becomes a loosely connected series of events, with no enduring subject or agent to whom authorship of action can be attributed. Yet the more we think about this, the more it starts to look like a fantasy of evasion. We cannot, however much we may wish to, escape responsibility for our actions; there is no way, ultimately, of sidestepping the requirement to give an account of the choices we made yesterday in the light of how they have turned out for ourselves and for others today.

This connects with a basic intuition found in Aristotle—that a good human life must be understood and evaluated as a whole, and that the virtues necessary for a good life cannot be fully present in isolation, but must be somehow integrated or interconnected.[40] Aristotle insists that *eudaimonia*, human fulfilment or flourishing, has to be measured *over a whole lifetime*.[41] Here Aristotle's account of flourishing draws analogies between the good for humankind and the good for any other biological species. For a plant to flourish is for it to grow, slowly and steadily, towards an end-state. And similarly, in the words of an earlier and very different text, which nevertheless captures something of the spirit of Aristotle, a good man is "like a tree planted by streams of water, which yields its fruit in season and whose leaf does not wither—whatever he does prospers."[42] There is a rhythm, a growth towards perfection, and this unfolds over time, over the complete lifespan of the organism. So it is not just a matter of adding up the various satisfying activities undertaken during our

40. Aristotle, *Nicomachean Ethics*, bk. 6, ch. 13.
41. *En biō teleiō*; Aristotle, bk. 1, ch. 7, 1098a18.
42. Psalm 1:3.

lifetime: there is more to the flourishing life than a mere aggregate of separate valuable activities. There needs to be an overall teleological pattern,[43] and the various virtues or excellences needed to realize this pattern all need to fit harmoniously together; for Aristotle insists on a holistic conception of virtue where the possession of one virtue implies the possession of them all.[44] In short, the good life for Aristotle has an *organic unity*. There is something that the human being is meant to be—a unified, flourishing organism, developing its characteristic and interrelated excellences over a complete lifetime.[45]

This also connects with an idea found in many religious traditions, that we are not self-creating beings, and hence that in order to be meaningful, our lives must be directed towards what is already laid down as objectively good for humankind, rather than being a function of isolated individual or collectively determined choice or desire. To the champions of creativity or the advocates of the happy-go-lucky life, such ideas can appear stifling and constricting. But the idea of the meaningful life as "integrated" does not mean everyone has to lead the same kind of existence: there is clearly room for many varieties of human flourishing, including very creative ones, such as the life of the intellectual, the artist, the musician, and so on. To constitute a truly meaningful life, however, these varied activities cannot be driven merely by a desire for personal or even collective satisfaction. Whether or not it is explicitly articulated, there has to be a sense of the worthwhile part they play in the story of the growth

43. Not to have your life planned towards some end, says Aristotle, is a "sign of great folly"; *Eudemian Ethics*, 1214b10–11.

44. Aristotle, *Nicomachean Ethics*, bk. 6, ch. 13, 1145a1–2.

45. For a development of this idea that goes beyond Aristotle's framework, see Cottingham, "Happiness, Temporality, Meaning."

and flowering of the individual agent, and of the other human agents with which that story is necessarily intertwined. In short, the reflective human agent cannot be content with a compartmentalized or haphazard life, but must seek to shape her life around an intelligible pattern, one which recognizes that her individuality can only operate within relationships of mutuality, which learns from past mistakes, and, above all, which strives to integrate her various pursuits into the pursuit of the good, and so make that life complete.

The underlying idea is finely expressed in George Eliot's novel *Silas Marner*. Though not a "religious" work in any conventional sense (at the time of writing Eliot had long abandoned any doctrinal allegiance to the Christian faith in which she had been brought up), the book nevertheless carries unmistakeable signs of a deeply felt moral and spiritual outlook, which is, inevitably, shaped by the faith of her childhood. At the start of the second half of the novel, where the story resumes after an interval of sixteen years, we revisit the small rural community of Raveloe that is the main setting for the narrative, and encounter once more one of the protagonists, Nancy Lammeter, who during the intervening period has left her girlhood behind and got married:

> Perhaps the pretty woman . . . is more changed than her husband: the lovely bloom that used to be always on her cheek now comes but fitfully, with fresh morning air or with some strong surprise; yet to all who love human faces best for what they tell of human experience, Nancy's beauty has a heightened interest. Often *the soul is ripened into fuller goodness* while age has spread an ugly film, so that mere glances can never divine the preciousness of the fruit.[46]

46. Eliot, *Silas Marner*, ch. 16, 137, emphasis added.

Nancy has not merely changed physically or entered a later phase of her life. Time has matured her, but it is not simply that her appearance has altered, or that her pursuits and interests have moved on. All this may be true, but what Eliot chooses to underline is that there has been a *ripening of the soul*. Nancy's qualities, as the novel will subsequently make clear, have been tested; and in that testing there has been a moral growth, a flowering of all that is best in her nature, a "ripening into fuller goodness," so that this one frail individual human life has been able to yield, over time, the "precious fruit" that it had the potential to bring forth.

We are here brought back full circle to one of the themes broached at the start of this chapter: the notion of the human soul as the true self that represents the best that each of us can become; the moral core of our being, whose loss is the greatest risk we can incur, and whose preservation and fostering are the key to our moral and psychological health and well-being.

But Why the Soul?

Even if one accepts the notion of a unified life, integrated around an objective conception of the good, as something to which human beings ought to aspire, many may still feel qualms about expressing this goal as one of finding or looking after the *soul*. For however natural it may have been in the past to talk of the human soul, and even though the term may still have some currency in certain utopian or poetic contexts, the idea of "soul" seems far less at home in our contemporary culture than it once was. To many people, the most authoritative and reliable way of understanding ourselves and our relation to the world is via the methods of science; and science, it seems, no longer has any use for entities like "souls." As already mentioned in the previous section, the concept of the soul to many people has "Platonic" overtones, suggesting that we human beings can somehow gain access to such a supra-sensible world, perhaps in virtue of having, in addition to our biological nature, some sort of immaterial or spiritual nature. All these ideas run counter to the prevailing philosophical doctrine known as *naturalism*, according to which there is no ultimate reality apart from the empirical world studied by science.

Many complex questions are raised here, but what can be said straight off is that science, for all its magnificent achievements, could never be shown to have provided a complete and final account of all reality: those who suppose otherwise have stepped outside science and fallen for the seductive dogma of *scientism*, whose incoherencies are well established. Scientism, the claim that science is the measure of *all* of reality, or *all* truth, is a claim that could not possibly be established by scientific means, and therefore, if truly asserted, would be self-refuting. The point was vividly put many decades ago by the British philosopher Paul Grice:

> We must be ever watchful against the devil of scientism, who would lead us into myopic overconcentration on the nature and importance of knowledge, and of scientific knowledge in particular; . . . who is even so audacious as to tempt us to call in question the very system of ideas required to make intelligible the idea of calling in question anything at all; and who would even prompt us, in effect, to suggest that since we do not really think but only think that we think, we had better change our minds without undue delay.[47]

A blanket philosophical prejudice against entities not ultimately reducible to the categories accepted by science is hard to justify.

47. Grice, "Method in Philosophical Psychology," 53.

But in any case, and leaving aside for a moment the tenability or otherwise of scientific naturalism, employing the concept of the soul *does not necessarily commit one to a belief in immaterial or supra-sensible entities.* There are philosophical theories of the soul, as we shall explore in the next chapter, which do not treat the soul as a separate immaterial entity, but on the contrary hold that the capacities associated with the soul are rooted in, and dependent on, suitably organized biological systems.[48]

Nevertheless, the tendency for the march of science to marginalize or erode the acceptability of the term "soul" cannot be denied. The Greek term for soul, *psyche*, became, in effect, appropriated during the nineteenth century by the newly burgeoning science of the mind. And the gradually emerging disciplines of psychology and psychiatry (etymologically, the "study of the soul" and the "cure of the soul") had little apparent connection with the "soul" in the sense in which the term had often been used in religious contexts (in reference, for example, to personal immortality), let alone with the idea of the soul as an immaterial mental substance.[49] Instead, in the case of psychology, the subject matter had to do with the empirical scientific study of the workings of the human and animal mind, manifested in desire, aversion, appetition, memory, sensation, cognition, and so on, together with the relevant behavioural dispositions, while psychiatry became part of medical science, dealing with diagnosis and treatment of various disorders of those same faculties.

The subsequent practitioners of these disciplines have often tended to embrace a materialistic world view that has little time for "souls"; and this is even more true of the more recent and

48. See ch. 2, "What Is the Soul?" below.
49. See below on Descartes, ch. 2, "Descartes and the Shrinking Soul."

rapidly expanding fields of cognitive science and neuroscience, which are seen as having the goal of explaining all aspects of human mental activity by reference to the functioning of the brain. The philosopher Daniel Dennett, perhaps the best known champion of this burgeoning science of the mind, puts the matter uncompromisingly:

> The total set of details of heterophenomenology [data gathered from people's reports about their conscious experiences], plus all the data we can gather about concurrent events in the brains of subjects and in the surrounding environment, comprise the total data set for a theory of human consciousness. It leaves out no objective phenomena and no subjective phenomena of consciousness.[50]

There are two issues here that need to be carefully distinguished. One is the question of whether our human mental functions and faculties are grounded or realized in physical processes and structures (such as brain circuitry) as opposed to some immaterial entity or force. And on this question, there is a massive accumulation of data (for example, from brain scans) that seems clearly to confirm that human thought and cognition are intimately dependent on neuroelectrical and chemical processes in the brain. But Dennett's declaration, quoted above, that *nothing is left out*, once we have gathered data about these brain processes, and correlated them with facts about the surrounding environment and people's reports of what they are experiencing, is much more problematic. Elsewhere Dennett has compared the modern scientific study of consciousness with other physical sciences such as meteorology: once you have achieved a theory that explains all the phenomena, "you

---

50. Dennett, "Who's On First?"

get to declare victory: you've finished the task because that is all there is to explain."[51]

But there *is* more to explain; or if not to "explain" in scientific terms, there is at least more to understand and to take account of. Dennett's enumeration of the "total data set" that defines what needs to be explained in constructing a "theory of consciousness" airily declares itself to be complete and comprehensive: it cannot on his view be charged with "leaving out" anything, presumably because there is no question of it needing to include scientifically dubious items like the "subjective phenomena of consciousness." But this appears to ignore the entire rich web of mental activity manifest to each conscious subject as a complex flow of beliefs and desires, feelings and sensations, aspirations and longings—everything that gives our existence *meaning*. Each of us can truly say that we have a sense of ourselves as unique subjects of experience, looking out onto the world from a horizon that no one else can cross, yet at the same time able to interact with other subjects, to offer them reasons for our actions, and reciprocally, to respond to the reasons they offer for theirs; and from this is derived the whole precious network of intersubjectivity that structures our human lives.

It is fundamentally misguided to suppose that the web of meaning arising from this human mental activity—our thoughts and feelings and hopes and fears—can be reduced to the working of brain processes. Meaning and interpretation require a whole context of social organization and interpersonal communication, a rich culture and "form of life," the understanding of which takes us far outside the scope of psychological and neurological science, however sophisticated. So while welcoming the scientific advances in neurobiology, one can still find

51. See Papineau, "Papineau vs Dennett."

scope for retaining a "domain of the soul." This need not imply any necessary commitment to the existence of strange immaterial entities, but will simply denote our human ability to access a realm of meaning and value, manifest, for example, in our artistic and literary and moral and religious experience (not to mention the theorizings and models and metaphors developed by the scientists themselves!). In all of these domains there is rich and irreducible content that is simply of a different kind from the phenomena falling within the scope of scientific inquiry.

Part of that domain of meaning and value is alluded to in ordinary non-philosophical uses of the term "soul," as in the poetic and other examples we have been discussing earlier, when the soul is said to be nourished, or exalted, by experiences that have deep significance for our lives.[52] No doubt brain events are going on when such experiences occur—how could they not be? But anyone who supposes that in pointing to a presentation slide of parts of the brain "lighting up" they are on the way to a complete explanation of such experiences is allowing their commendable zeal for science to occlude the palpable evidence of their own introspective awareness—even driving them to insist (as one increasingly finds in much recent cognitive science literature) that this awareness is an "illusion."[53]

To be human is to have an inner life. This need not mean that we have immaterial powers, or that our consciousness is not dependent on brain activity. But it does mean that there is more to the task of understanding ourselves than the language and methods of science could ever encompass. Such understanding cannot be gained wholly "from the outside," from the objective methods of empirical observation and scientific measurement,

52. "Dimensions of Soul," above.
53. I shall return to the "illusionist" approach to consciousness in ch. 3.

but must involve reference to the "interior" or subjective dimension. This does not mean we can dispense with the help of others: we were not made for solipsistic isolation, and indeed we could not function properly as human beings in the first place except as part of a community of others whom we immediately recognize and respond to as "ensouled," just as we are. When I encounter another human being, as Ludwig Wittgenstein remarked, I am not *of the opinion* that he has a soul; instead, immediately and without inference, "my attitude towards him is an attitude towards a soul."[54] What is more, our ability to respond to other human beings in this way is of profound ethical importance for the task that confronts us all of growing towards the selves we were meant to be. Nevertheless, this is a task that can be undertaken only by the *experiencing subject*, by what Descartes called "this *me* [*ce moi*], that is to say the soul, by which I am what I am."[55] Descartes may have been mistaken in identifying this "soul" with a ghostly incorporeal substance (we shall look at that question in the next chapter); but one does not have to accept an immaterialist view of the soul in order to accept the irreducible reality of the experiencing subject—"this *me* . . . by which I am what I am."

We are all engaged in the task of trying to understand the "soul" in this sense: the experiencing subject, the core self that makes us what we are. What is more, the soul or self that is both the individual subject undertaking this task and the object that each of us seeks to understand, and whose growth and maturity we seek to foster in ourselves and encourage in others, is not a static or closed phenomenon. Each of us, like it or not, is on a

54. Wittgenstein, *Philosophical Investigations*, pt. 2, sec. 4, 178.
55. Descartes, *Discourse on the Method*, pt. 4, AT, vol. 6, 33; CSM, vol. 1, 127. See below, ch. 2, "Descartes and the Shrinking Soul."

journey, to grow and to learn, and to reach towards the best that we can become. We have to understand ourselves teleologically, as striving towards whatever can lift us above the waste and futility of our failures and inadequacies and draw us towards something we recognize as having transcendent value and importance. In addressing this task we aim to realize our true selves. This is what the task of "finding the soul" amounts to; and it is here, if there is a meaning to human life, that such meaning must be sought.

2

The Evolution of the Soul

The Soul is placed in the Body like a rough Diamond, and must be polish'd, or the lustre of it will never appear.

—DANIEL DEFOE, *AN ESSAY UPON PROJECTS*

What Is the Soul?

"Do you think you have a soul?" In the light of some of the issues raised in the previous chapter, such a question may produce a kind of mental cramp. On the one hand, we may feel the force of the modern scientific impulse to dispense with occult or "spooky" notions like souls and spirits, and to understand ourselves instead as wholly and completely part of the natural world, existing and operating through the same physical and chemical and biological processes that we find anywhere else in the environment. But on the other hand, we immediately recognize and respond to what the poets are saying when they speak of the "soul" in connection with certain powerful and transforming experiences, of love for our fellow creatures, for example, or of wonder at the beauties of nature. And when religious writers speak of "gaining the world but losing one's soul," we intuitively grasp what is meant by the loss in question—the kind of moral disorientation and collapse where what is true and good slips out of our grasp and we find we have wasted our lives on some specious gain that is ultimately worthless.

Part of the problem here is that we are caught between a scientifically driven way of interpreting the question "do you have a soul?"—a framework in terms of which many people might be perfectly happy to reply in the negative—and a morally or spiritually oriented understanding of "soul," according to which most of us would like to be able to say that yes, we do indeed have a soul. For we do recognize something deep within us that responds to the good and the noble, and despite all our failures we still aspire to deepen and develop that responsive part of us and to make it central to who we are. In this moral and spiritual sense, reluctant though we may sometimes be to admit it, we all want to "find ourselves," as the saying goes—to discover, and to live up to, our true moral identity; and so in this sense we already understand something of what is meant by the task of "finding the soul."

Are we dealing with two completely separate questions here—a factual or scientific question, about the explanation and physical basis of our human mental capacities, and a moral question about the good for humankind and how we ought to live? In some ways, from our contemporary perspective, it is natural to keep these two questions in distinct and separate compartments—compartments labelled "fact" and "value" respectively; but there are philosophical risks in allowing all of our thinking to be conditioned by this standard dichotomy. As far as the "soul" is concerned, it is instructive to compare our modern ways of looking at these issues with earlier philosophical frameworks, where the very idea of a rigid separation between "fact" and "value" would not have made much sense. For if we go back to the classical era, we find that both Plato and Aristotle discuss the notion of soul—or in Greek, *psyche*—in terms that inextricably mix together "factual" questions about the properties and capacities of the human mind (sensation, belief, thought, feeling, rationality, and so on) with "moral" questions about the good for human beings or the human good—*to anthrōpinon agathon*, to use Aristotle's phrase.[1]

The original root of the Greek term *psyche* connects with the verb for to breathe or blow. There is something similar in the Hebrew Bible, where the Hebrew word for spirit, *ruach*, has the literal meaning of "breath," and is found in the phrase "the breath of life." Elsewhere, in the Genesis creation story, God is said to breathe into the nostrils of man so that he becomes a living *soul* (*nephesh*).[2] Without going into the detailed etymology of the various words involved, the general idea in both languages might be construed in very simple terms: breathing is a characteristic manifestation of life, and when a human being dies the immediate and obvious difference observed is that breath ceases. So the soul is initially thought of as the "breath of life"—that which makes the difference between a living human being and a corpse. The same basic idea is found in Latin, where *anima* (normally translated "soul") originally meant a wind, current of air, or breath.

Psyche in Greek thus refers in a broad sense to the principle responsible for life: if something is *empsychos* ("ensouled"), it is alive, functioning, animate as opposed to inanimate. But life takes many forms, and for Aristotle the various functions found in living things form a hierarchy. A living plant grows and takes in nourishment, but a living animal also manifests additional functions—locomotion and sensation, for instance. Aristotle expresses this by saying that plants have a "nutritive soul," and animals have, in addition, a "locomotive soul." What he means is that, in each case, the various biological structures and organs

1. Aristotle, *Nicomachean Ethics*, bk. 1, ch. 7.
2. Genesis 2:7.

are configured so as to allow the relevant faculties to work. And finally, in the case of human beings, there is a "rational soul," responsible for reasoning and thinking.[3]

But bound alongside with this seemingly rather factual and biological conception of soul is what might be called a *normative* conception. Being "ensouled," even in the relatively simple case of a plant, is not just a matter of physical mechanisms happening to operate, but involves the physical parts being ordered or configured in such a way as to facilitate the good and healthy functioning of the organism in question. In this sense the soul is, as Aristotle puts it, the *form* of the body—a principle whereby the body is configured so as to actualize its potentiality and enable it to function (grow, move, have sensations, think and reason), and thus realize the good that is appropriate to its nature.

For both Plato and Aristotle there are necessary and intimate connections between something's specific function (in Greek, *ergon*), and the good for that thing: "in the function lies the good" (*en tō ergō to agathon*).[4] And both philosophers see the good for humankind as involving the functioning of the rational part that is the special distinguishing characteristic of human beings. In a famous simile used by Plato in the *Phaedrus*, the soul is compared to a chariot, with reason as the driver, and two horses pulling it, a dark one representing the various desires and appetites and a lighter one representing the more spirited emotions (such as courage). The image has been variously interpreted, and some see it as looking forward to the Stoic idea of the complete governance of reason and the suppression of the passions, while others see it as a more harmonious vision in

3. Aristotle, *De Anima*, bk. 2, ch. 4.
4. Aristotle, *Nicomachean Ethics*, bk. 1, ch. 7, 1097b; cf. Plato, *Republic*, bk. 1, 352–54.

which the various parts of the soul work together, the unruly desires needing to be curbed, while the nobler and more spirited desires are natural allies of reason, although still requiring a guiding hand. The interpretation of Plato is a complex matter, but the prevailing impression in many key Platonic texts—the *Republic* is a notable example—is of the best life, the life of philosophical reason, operating on a pure, rational plane, as far as possible free from the distortions arising from the murky world of the senses and emotions and bodily appetites.[5]

The influence of Plato can be seen in his pupil Aristotle, insofar as Aristotle's *Nicomachean Ethics* culminates with a vision of the highest good as consisting in a life of reason in the sense of abstract theoretical contemplation. But Aristotle tellingly adds that "such a life will be too high for human attainment, for any man who lives it will do so not as a human being but in virtue of something divine within him."[6] The bulk of Aristotle's ethics is devoted instead to a much more down-to-earth conception of human flourishing, where the emotions play a key role in the pattern of right feeling and right action that marks out the virtuous person. In other words, the good life involves the full flowering of our humanity in all its dimensions, not an exclusive focus on the activities of the intellect. This contrast between the Platonic and Aristotelian approaches to ethics should not be overdone: a more detailed look at the relevant writings would reveal a much more complicated picture, with many areas of overlap. But for our present purposes, the difference in emphasis between the two thinkers is of interest because it connects with a significant difference in how they understood the notion of *psyche*, or soul.

5. Plato, *Republic*, bk. 6, 484–87.
6. Aristotle, *Nicomachean Ethics*, bk. 10, ch. 7.

Out of This World?

The idea of the soul as distinct from or contrasted with the body is a recurring theme in Western philosophy, and it receives much of its impetus from Plato. In Plato's dialogue the *Phaedo*, which depicts the last days of Socrates after his condemnation by an Athenian court, Socrates is involved in a long discussion of what happens to us when we die:

> After a man is dead, the body, or visible part of him, which is in the visible world and is called a corpse, will naturally be dissolved and decompose. . . . But the soul which is pure at departing and carries no taint of the body . . . the soul, I say, which is itself invisible, departs towards the invisible world, to the divine and immortal and rational, and when it arrives there it is sure of happiness.[7]

So the soul is that part of us that is invisible and immortal and which will survive the death of the body. Elsewhere in the dialogue, Socrates famously characterizes human life as a "preparation for dying": the goal of our existence is to purify the soul from its damaging attachment to the body and ready it for the pure, rational activity that is its ultimate destiny.[8] On this dualistic view, which has powerfully influenced so much subsequent thinking, the deterioration of the body over time is not ultimately anything much to regret, since it brings us nearer to our proper destination—the eventual separation of soul from body. Indeed, the infirmities of old age would seem, on this dualistic view, to be a help, not a hindrance, in the

7. Plato, *Phaedo*, 80b–81c.
8. Plato, *Phaedo*, 67e.

necessary Socratic process of learning to despise the bodily pleasures and attachments that hinder the functioning of the immortal part of us.

The purity and austerity of the Platonic position (vividly reinforced in the *Phaedo* by the dramatic and moving account of the noble death of Socrates) presents many problems. For one thing, the crucial activities attributed by Plato to the soul, such as philosophical reasoning and theoretical contemplation, are self-evidently *not* facilitated or increased by the increasing decrepitude of the body. On the contrary, ordinary observation, supported by a plethora of medical and scientific evidence, clearly indicates that intellectual activity is characteristically diminished in varying degrees by the infirmities of ageing, and in the case of some specific conditions (Alzheimer's disease or severe stroke, for instance) is curtailed, or even eliminated altogether. So, far from its being something independent of the body, what Plato calls the soul, with its characteristic rational and intellectual capacities, seems intimately bound up with the functioning of the body, and especially the nervous system and the brain.[9]

A Platonic-style soul-body dualist might perhaps argue that the activity of the soul is not actually being damaged or eradicated in cases of bodily disease or decay, but simply subjected to swamping or interference from distracting bodily signals (rather as the operation of a television might be temporarily impaired by a cracked circuit board without its losing its pristine power to do its job perfectly once the damage is repaired).[10] But

9. See further Cottingham, "Question of Ageing."

10. Cf. Richard Swinburne's defence of traditional substance dualism in *Evolution of the Soul*.

the analogy seems of very limited value in supporting the Platonic claim that the soul's rational powers could still function *without any physical vehicle whatever*. Both in the case of an inanimate object like a television and also in any biological case we can think of, structure and function seem to be intimately related. It doesn't make much sense to think that the cutting function of a knife could float free of the physical structure (e.g., a sharpened blade) that allows this function to be performed. It doesn't make much sense to think of the functions of seeing, or hearing, or smelling somehow surviving the destruction of the eyes and ears and olfactory organs that enable these functions to operate. We could perhaps imagine doctors constructing artificial structures to replace damaged organs (indeed, such devices are already being developed by modern medical science); but to think of the functions operating in an invisible and immaterial realm, without any material substrate whatever, seems to verge on the unintelligible.

In contrast to this, Aristotle's general position on human nature, in the light of his famous definition of the human being as a "rational *animal*," seems considerably more "body-friendly" than Plato's: our biological or corporeal nature, on the Aristotelian account, is an essential part of what we are. In the first book of his *De anima* (On the Soul), Aristotle says that the way people often speak about "souls" has something absurd about it. For there are various philosophers who "tack the soul on to the body," or locate it *in* the body, but they give no account of what the condition of the body must be like for this to be possible. The relation between soul and body, Aristotle goes on to say, surely cannot be a purely contingent or haphazard one. So when the Pythagoreans, for example, talk of "metempsychosis," the transmigration of souls, this is nonsense, since it suggests that any soul could flit into any body:

The Pythagorean stories suggest that any soul can find its way into any body, which is absurd; for we can see that every body has its own special shape or form. The Pythagorean view is like suggesting that carpentry can find its way into flutes. But each craft must employ its own tools, and each soul its own body.[11]

In other words, each body or physical structure has a characteristic form or shape that enables it to perform the relevant functions. *Structure and function are intimately related,* so that the job done by a saw or a hammer requires tools of a certain shape and strength—it would be absurd to say the function could float away and be embodied in a different physical object like a flute.

All this is a perfectly straightforward consequence of Aristotle's down-to-earth theory of the soul, known somewhat portentously as *hylemorphism* (from the Greek *hylē*, matter, and *morphē*, form). The soul is not a separate entity in its own right, but is related to body as form is to matter, or as organizing principle is to material constitution, or as function is to structure. To follow up Aristotle's analogy, *formally* speaking, a flute is an instrument whose job is to produce a series of characteristic high-pitched, breathy piping sounds; and in order to instantiate this form, the *material* has to be constructed out of a tube made of metal or something similar, with holes or stops and a mouthpiece shaped so that the player's breath can strike a narrow edge. For this reason, the "soul" (in inverted commas) of a flute couldn't migrate into the body of a trombone, still less into a chisel or a hammer, nor for that matter could the "soul" of a chisel migrate into the body of a hammer. The relation between the activity being performed and the structure of the relevant materials is not

11. Aristotle, *De anima*, bk. 1, ch. 3.

a haphazard one, but is tightly constrained by the specification of the form—the design specification, if you like—and the suitability of the materials, properly configured, to execute this design.

This Aristotelian line of thought about the relation between body and soul has proved remarkably durable, and has seemed to a number of philosophers in our own day to offer the basis for a credible and attractive middle way between radical materialism on the one hand (the attempt to reduce all mental phenomena to purely physical properties or events), and substance dualism (the introduction of a Platonic-style, "pure" incorporeal soul) on the other.[12] The great twentieth-century philosopher Ludwig Wittgenstein may have been quite close to thinking along Aristotelian lines when he declared *"Der menschliche Körper ist das beste Bild der menschlichen Seele"*—"the human body is the best picture of the human soul."[13] Though the remark underlines the importance of the body, Wittgenstein is not, any more than Aristotle, espousing some kind of crude behaviourism or materialistic reductionism. Instead, the point seems to be that we see the soul of the pianist, for example, in the sensitivity and flexibility of her fingers, in the movements of her body and the expression on her face as she plays, indeed in the whole way in which she engages in the very physical process of playing the piano; and there's no doubt much more that we can't normally see, in the way the nerves and sinews and brain are configured so as to make all this possible.

The more we think about this, the less sense we can make of the idea of the concert pianist's soul transmigrating to another body (the body of a sumo wrestler, for example), let alone

12. For an impressive recent example, see Jaworski, *Metaphysics of Mind*.
13. Wittgenstein, *Philosophical Investigations*, pt. 2, sec. 4.

continuing to function in complete separation from any bodily structure. For the soul, on Aristotle's view, though it is not to be *identified* with the body, is nevertheless intimately related to the body. The soul is, in the Aristotelian phrase, a "principle involving matter"; and, conversely, the matter of which the body is composed has to be "ensouled" or "in-formed" in a particular way in order for the individual in question to be alive and operating and functioning.

So is the Platonic idea of a "pure," incorporeal soul just a confusion, or mere wishful thinking—part of the age-old longing of human beings to be free from physical constraints and from the inexorable processes of decay and mortality? That there may be more to it than that is suggested by the passage from the *Phaedo* with which we began, where the immortal realm where the soul is supposed to survive after the body's death is described by Plato as the realm of the *rational*. Part of the thought seems to be that our powers of rational understanding are radically different from our powers of sensation and appetite, which have an obvious connection with the body. When we exercise our reason, we escape from the sense-bound world and consider more timeless, abstract properties—logical relations, for instance, or mathematical ideas, or universal essences. We enter a realm that in a certain way *transcends* the physical and the temporal; the mind or soul can in this sense be thought of as an "instrument of transcendence."[14] And hence the Platonist finds it reasonable to suppose that just as the *objects* we focus on are timeless abstract objects, outside the contingent and empirical world of our ordinary sensory experience, so too the *faculty*, the intellectual part of us that enables us to access or contemplate these objects, is

14. Nagel, *Mind and Cosmos*, 85. We shall return to this idea in the final chapter.

itself somehow a transcendent faculty, able to operate independently of bodily constraints, free from the "taint" of the body, as Plato puts it.

If this is part of the underlying philosophical rationale for belief in an immaterial soul, it may in classical times have seemed to draw support from the fact that there is no obvious bodily organ of the intellect, in the way, for instance, that there are obvious physical organs of sight and the other senses. Even by the seventeenth century, as we shall see in a moment, there was little or no grasp of the role of the cerebral cortex, or of its staggering neural complexity. So the apparent absence of a physical organ of the intellect may for the ancient Greek thinkers have reinforced the idea that there is something "invisible" and immaterial about our intellectual and rational faculties. The point may indeed have swayed Aristotle, despite his normal "hylemorphic" framework, since he does not entirely succeed in sticking to this framework when it comes to the powers of the intellect. The standard hylemorphic idea, as already indicated, is that we can give a formal or functional description of our powers and capacities (hearing, for instance, is the capacity to detect and discriminate sounds), but that these capacities always have to be instantiated in or realized by physical structures (such as the outer and middle and inner ear), which are "formed" or configured in such a way as to allow this function to operate. So *both* the "formal" *and* the material are essential aspects of understanding what hearing is (and the same goes for other sensory functions). But when it comes to intellect, Aristotle hesitates on whether it may not after all be able to function in separation from the body:

> The soul is the source of [the various functions found in plants and animals] and is defined by the faculties of nutrition,

perception, thought and movement. But . . . concerning the
intellect and the capacity for contemplation, the situation is
not so far clear, but it seems to be a different kind of soul; it
may be that it alone can exist separately, as the everlasting can
exist in separation from the perishable. But the other parts of
the soul are not separable.[15]

So both Plato and Aristotle seem to end up agreeing that "a
certain kind of soul" (as Aristotle puts it)—namely, the intellectual and rational part of us—may be somehow separable
from the body, and capable of surviving the biological decay
and destruction that awaits us all. As will be seen, this idea of a
separable and immaterial soul was to receive a fresh impetus at
the start of the modern age.

From Souls to Ghosts

From the brief survey just offered of the Platonic and Aristotelian accounts of the soul, a tension between the two approaches
is clearly apparent. In Plato, the soul turns out to be something
essentially distinct from the body, and capable of surviving the
body's destruction, while for Aristotle the general picture (albeit with reservations about the intellectual part of us) is of soul
and body as different aspects of one and the same living human
organism. This tension in the legacy from the classical era continued to exercise the minds of the great medieval philosophers,
notably Thomas Aquinas, who based many of his ideas on an
Aristotelian framework, but who set himself the task of recon-
ciling the principles of Aristotle's philosophy with the doctrines
of Christianity. What we find in Aquinas is a somewhat uneasy

15. Aristotle, *De anima*, bk. 3, ch. 3.

compromise between a broadly Aristotelian account of the faculties of the soul as "principles involving matter," and a more "separatist" or Platonic conception—one that is perhaps better suited to the Christian doctrine of a future state in which the soul will continue after the body's death, awaiting final reunion with the body at the resurrection. Thus for Aquinas the parts of the soul responsible for sensation and nutrition belong to the human being as a "composite" of soul and body; but the higher faculties of intellect and will "belong to the soul alone," and hence will remain in the soul after the destruction of the body.[16]

Despite his Platonic-sounding commitment to the idea of an immortal soul that could be separated from the body, Aquinas continued to consider the soul in Aristotelian terms, as the "form" of the body, and therefore as something that, considered on its own, is essentially *incomplete*. My soul, for Aquinas, is not the whole me: *anima mea non est ego*.[17] Francisco Suarez, one of the most noted followers of Aquinas in the Renaissance, summed up this view when he said that "a soul, even if it separated, is always an incomplete substance."[18] Another Thomistic philosopher of the period, Eustachius, put it like this:

> Separated souls are *not*, like angels, whole subjects that are totally and in every respect complete. . . . A soul, even when

16. Aquinas, *Summa theologiae*, pt. 1, qu. 75, art. 6, and pt. 1, qu. 77, art. 5: "Some operations that belong to the soul are carried out through bodily organs, such as seeing (through the eye) and hearing (through the ear), and likewise for all other operations of the nutritive or sensitive part. Hence the powers that are the sources of such operations *are in the compound as their subject, not in the soul alone*" (emphasis added).

17. Thomas Aquinas, *Commentarium super Epistolam I ad Corinthos* [Commentary on First Letter to the Corinthians], ch. 15, verses 12–19; cited in Davies, *Thomas Aquinas*, 23.

18. Suarez, *Metaphysical Disputations*, disp. 33, sec. 1, para. 11.

separated, is always apt to inform the body and to be substantially united with it.[19]

To help us understand these remarks about the incompleteness of the "separated" human soul after death, it is worth remembering that the Christian idea of the afterlife centres on the idea of bodily resurrection, as opposed to a purely incorporeal existence. "I believe in the resurrection of the body," says the Apostles' Creed, *not* "I believe in the survival of an immaterial soul." For the scholastic followers of Aquinas, the human soul was *not* thought of as a kind of pure, incorporeal spirit, like an angel, but rather as something incomplete, something that always in principle needs to be united with the body that it "informs" for its essential completion. Thus the souls in purgatory are conceived of as existing in a kind of suspended state, awaiting— indeed, requiring as their very *raison d'être*—restoration to human status, when they will be rejoined to the body at the last judgement.

In our own contemporary culture, the notion of the soul, insofar as most people think about it at all, sometimes seems to carry faint echoes of these earlier conceptions. But what do people nowadays really mean when after a funeral, for example, once the bodily remains have been buried or cremated, they say "May his *soul* rest in peace"? No doubt there are theologians who might be prepared to offer an answer. But if one were to do a random survey, asking people what kind of thing a soul is, or what sort of image the term conjures up, one suspects there would be no very clear response. Occasionally one still hears talk about "departed spirits," and one can even find people who claim to communicate

---

19. Eustachius, *Summa philosophiae quadripartita*, pt. 3, third part, treatise 4, discourse 3, qu. 1.

with those who have "passed on." And in the séances that used to be a popular pastime in the early twentieth century, such spirits were sometimes supposed to "manifest" themselves as ghostly presences, composed of some kind of strange, immaterial "ectoplasm."[20] If this is what a "soul" or "spirit" has become in popular culture, we have come a long way from Aristotle's hylemorphism, the soul as "the form of the body," and even from Plato's idea of the rational part of us as destined for immortality. Instead, the soul seems to be thought of as a kind of ghost, a vague ethereal presence of someone who has "departed this life" that may sometimes return to communicate with us, or haunt us. If a soul is really a kind of ghost, it is something that many hardheaded sceptics would regard as a piece of nonsense, either a relic of primitive superstition or, worse, a cruel mockery invoked by the unscrupulous to prey on the misery of the bereaved.

The term "ghost," with its pejorative connotations to the modern mind, recalls Gilbert Ryle's label "the ghost in the machine," which he used to denounce Descartes's theory of the immaterial mind or soul.[21] Ryle's own theory of the mind was a form of behaviourism which does not win much support today; but partly as a result of his targeting of Descartes, the phrase "Cartesian dualism" has become, for many contemporary philosophers,

20. A belief in such "psychic phenomena" was for a time fashionable in the early decades of the twentieth century, attracting even some scientifically oriented minds. See Arthur Conan Doyle, *The Coming of the Fairies* (London: Hodder and Stoughton, 1922), which enthusiastically describes the photographic evidence for the existence of the "Cottingley fairies." (It emerged many decades later that the photographs had been faked.)

21. The terms "mind" and "soul" are often used interchangeably by Descartes to refer to a thinking substance (*res cogitans*), or "that which thinks" (*id quod cogitat*): Descartes, *Meditations*, Seventh Replies, AT, vol. 7, 487; CSM, vol. 2, 329. For the phrase "ghost in the machine," see Ryle, *Concept of Mind*, ch. 1.

almost synonymous with the idea of the mind or soul as some kind of "spooky" entity, a putatively immaterial thinking substance that is mysteriously supposed to lodge in the body, or perhaps in the brain, and to interact with the mechanisms of the nervous system in a way that resists any kind of scientific investigation. Many scientifically oriented philosophers of mind now define their outlook in opposition to what they take to be this egregious error of "Cartesian dualism." Fairly typical here is the comment of the British philosopher David Papineau, when he declares his resolute opposition to what he calls "magical explanations": we should be "vigilant against crediting minds with supernatural powers," and should always try to find "naturalistic alternatives."[22] But was Descartes's account of the soul really no more than an explanatory dead end, relegating the mind to a ghostly, supernatural domain that blocks scientific progress?

Descartes and the Shrinking Soul

The curious thing about the demonizing of Cartesian dualism that has become widespread among philosophers and scientists in our own time is that Descartes himself has a good claim to have inaugurated the scientific study of the human psyche. For he was at pains to argue that many of the capacities and faculties traditionally ascribed to a "soul" were in fact capable of being understood in terms of the laws of physics.

Descartes's lasting contribution to science was that he realized that the route to progress was a mathematical and mechanical one. Though not wholly innovative (ancient Greek thinkers such as Pythagoras and Democritus had developed mathematical and

22. Papineau, "Papineau vs Dennett."

corpuscular approaches to explanation), in the context of the early-modern intellectual climate Descartes's scientific pro-gramme marked a decisive step forward. In place of the "forms" and "qualities" of his scholastic predecessors, concepts whose explanatory power was exceedingly limited, Descartes devel-oped a template for scientific explanation based on quantitative principles: a wide range of diverse phenomena could be sub-sumed under simple, mathematically expressible laws, where the values for the variables were the size, shape, and motion of the corpuscles out of which all the matter in the universe was composed. And the quantitatively describable mechanisms governing the physiology of the animal and human body were, in Descartes's vision, no different in principle from those oper-ating in any other part of the universe.

Descartes's Aristotelian predecessors (as we have just seen) dealt with the various functions of living creatures (nutrition, movement, sensation, and so on) by referring to organizational or formal principles such as the nutritive, locomotive, and sen-sory "souls." But in Descartes's scheme of things, there is no in-trinsic qualitative difference between animate and inanimate matter; so once one has identified the various mechanisms of the body, and seen how their working depends on the size, shape, and motion of the particles of which they are composed, there is no need to use the terminology of "souls" at all. In his early work on the nature of human beings, the *Traité de l'homme*, Des-cartes explains a whole range of human activities in terms of the workings of a self-moving machine, which like a "clock or an ar-tificial fountain or mill" has the power to operate purely in ac-cordance with its own internal principles, depending solely on the disposition of the relevant organs.[23] And he goes on to insist

23. Descartes, *Treatise on Man*, AT, vol. 11, 120; CSM, vol. 1, 99.

that in order to account for these activities and functions it is not necessary to posit any "sensitive or vegetative soul," of the kind favoured by his medieval and scholastic predecessors. In general, Descartes's presumption is that there is nothing "special" about biological processes and functions; there is, for example, no special "principle of life" apart from the internal fire of the heart—a fire which has the same nature as the fires to be found elsewhere in inanimate objects.[24]

Here is the remarkably extensive list of human functions that Descartes proposes to explain in this way, without any reference to soul:

> the digestion of food, the beating of the heart and arteries, the nourishment and growth of the limbs, respiration, waking and sleeping, the reception by the external sense organs of light, sounds, smells, tastes, heat and other such qualities, the imprinting of ideas of these qualities in the organ of the "common" sense and the imagination, the retention or stamping of these ideas in the memory, the internal movements of the appetites and passions, and finally the external movements of all the limbs which aptly follow both the actions and objects presented to the senses and also the passions and impressions found in the memory.[25]

To those who have been taught to condemn Descartes for his dualistic introduction of magical and "spooky" entities, it may be surprising to notice the complete absence here of any reference to an immaterial soul. What we find instead is a research

---

24. Descartes, *Treatise on Man*, AT, vol. 11, 202; CSM, vol. 1, 108.

25. Descartes, *Treatise on Man*, AT, vol. 11, 202; CSM, vol. 1, 108. The term "'common' sense" was used by Aristotelians to signify an internal sense that receives and coordinates the impressions coming in from the five external senses.

programme driven by the desire for transparent quantitative and mechanistic explanations of psychological phenomena: the Cartesian approach here is anything but "spooky" or "magical." The functions that Descartes proposes to explain *without* invoking any soul include not only functions belonging to the autonomic nervous system such as respiration and heartbeat, but also psychological functions like sense perception and memory. And also included in the list are passions and sensations like fear and hunger, and even voluntary actions such as running. Those of his contemporaries who were accustomed to use the traditional Aristotelian soul terminology later asked Descartes whether he really proposed to dispense with the "sensitive soul" when explaining, for example, a sheep catching sight of a wolf and running away. Not only did Descartes readily acknowledge that this was indeed his proposal, but he also insisted that, *in the case of humans too*, a purely mechanistic explanation, making no reference to the soul, was quite sufficient to explain even such waking actions as walking and singing, at least when they occur *"without the mind attending to them"* (*animo non advertente*).[26]

This last crucial qualification signals that Descartes's programme for eliminating the soul wherever possible stops abruptly when it comes to *conscious mental attention*. Here Descartes holds that it is indeed necessary to posit a soul; and employing the label used by the Aristotelians he calls this "the rational soul" (*l'âme raisonnable*).[27] What Descartes flags up as resistant to mechanistic explanation is the mind's *attending* to the walking or the singing that is going on. The label "*rational* soul" employed by Descartes here makes it clear that we are in the domain of intellectual and conceptual activity—as, for example,

26. Descartes, *Meditations*, Fourth Replies, AT, vol. 7, 230; CSM, vol. 2, 161.
27. Descartes, *Treatise on Man*, AT, vol. 11, 143; CSM, vol. 1, 102.

when I'm not just absent-mindedly walking down the country lane but am deliberately *focusing* on what I am doing, explicitly thinking or reflecting about it. The upshot of all this is that in comparison with his Aristotelian predecessors, the scope of the soul has been radically *shrunk* by Descartes, but it has not been eliminated altogether. Aristotle's "nutritive" and "locomotive" and "sensitive" souls are made redundant, but the "rational soul" remains. But why exactly did Descartes believe our human conceptual abilities were recalcitrant to physical explanation?

Cartesian Automata and the Creativity of Thought

Descartes's reflections on the limits of quantitative scientific explanation led him to develop a thought experiment that will have many resonances for those familiar with consciousness studies today: he considered how we might be able to distinguish a human replica, or automaton, from a genuine human being.[28] The term "automaton" in the seventeenth century did not have the connotations it has nowadays, but simply meant an object that did not need to be pushed around externally but could move "on its own," in virtue of some internal mechanism (e.g., clockwork). Modern philosophers of mind use the quasi-technical term "zombie" to mean a creature that behaves just like a human being but supposedly without any "inner awareness" (so that there is "nothing it is like" to be a zombie).[29] But

28. See Cottingham, "Cartesian Dualism" and "Descartes and . . . Consciousness."

29. See Nagel, "What Is It Like," and Kirk, "Zombies." The term "zombie" was brought into use in this special philosophical sense by David Chalmers, in "Problem of Consciousness." For more on the idea of "what it is like" to have conscious

Descartes's focus is rather different: for him, "automaton" simply means any self-moving device. What fascinated Descartes's generation about the new craze for machines and mechanisms, ranging from clocks to the elaborately contrived moving statues to be found in some of the fountains in the royal parks, was simply this: the complex sequences of movements, which to earlier generations might have appeared to manifest some kind of inner motive "force" or "spirit," could all be explained quite simply by reference to internal mechanical structure—cogs, levers, pipes, and the like. Descartes mentions as an example a statue of Neptune that would threaten with its trident the approaching onlooker who had unwittingly stepped on a pressure pad.[30]

Descartes compares mechanical automata to non-human animals, and observes that it would in principle be possible to mistake a cleverly contrived artificial automaton for a real dog or monkey. Yet we could never mistake an automaton, however ingenious, for a human being. Why not? Because, says Descartes, an automaton could never talk. But why is *speech* so important? Descartes's reasoning strikingly anticipates an argument developed in the twentieth century by Noam Chomsky,[31] and depends on Descartes's view that a non-human animal is essentially a machine, a stimulus-response device. You may be able to train a magpie to say "bonjour," Descartes observed to a correspondent, but the word will be a fixed response to an external stimulus causing a given change in the nervous system.[32] As

---

awareness, see the second and third paragraphs of the following section, "The Soul-Body Unit and Descartes's Trialism."

30. Descartes, *Treatise on Man*, AT, vol. 11, 130–32; CSM, vol. 1, 100–101.

31. Chomsky, *Language and Mind*.

32. Descartes, letter to Newcastle, 23 November 1646, AT, vol. 4, 574; CSMK, 303.

Descartes put it in his first published work, the *Discourse on the Method*:

> We can certainly conceive of a machine so constructed that it utters words ... corresponding to ... a change in its organs (e.g. if you touch it in one spot it asks what you want of it, and if you touch it in another spot it cries out that you are hurting it). But it is not conceivable that such a machine should produce arrangements of words so as to give an appropriately meaningful answer to whatever is said in its presence, as even the dullest of men can do.[33]

The point Descartes is highlighting here is that the human language user has the capacity to respond appropriately to an indefinite range of situations—a capacity that seems generically distinct from anything that could be produced by a finite system generating a set of outputs from a set of inputs. For Descartes, no purely physical system could possibly have the resources to generate the kind of genuine creativity and innovativeness that is displayed in human linguistic behaviour.

It is important, especially in the light of the modern disdain for Cartesian ways of thinking, to be aware of the considerations that influenced Descartes in coming to these conclusions about the limitations of a physical system. What made it reasonable to maintain that an automaton could not possibly trick us into thinking it was a genuine human being was, for Descartes, at least partly a matter of *number and size*—of how many structures of the appropriate kind could be packed into a given part of the body. For Descartes, the brain or nervous system was clearly physically unable to accommodate enough mechanisms

---

33. Descartes, *Discourse on the Method*, pt. 5, AT, vol. 6, 56–57; CSM, vol. 1, 140.

to generate the indefinitely large range of complex responses characteristic of the genuine thinker and language user:

> Since reason is a universal instrument which can be used in all kinds of situations, whereas [bodily] organs need some particular disposition for each particular action, it is morally impossible [*moralement impossible*—i.e., impossible for all practical purposes] for a machine to have enough different organs to make it act in all the contingencies of life in the way in which our reason makes us act.[34]

As a result of this "practical impossibility," Descartes was driven to suppose that the hidden schematism responsible for thought was an immaterial rational soul. But his "language argument" (that no automaton could produce genuine language) is very much empirically oriented: it hinges on the practical impossibility of a physical mechanism possessing a sufficiently large number of different parts to facilitate the indefinite range of human linguistic responses to "all the contingencies of life." Could such an argument survive the modern discovery of the unimaginable complex microstructure of the cerebral cortex, composed, as we now know, of over eighty-five billion neurons and a hundred trillion synaptic connections? Well, perhaps Descartes might still have maintained that a purely physical structure could not generate the relevant kind of plasticity and innovativeness necessary for genuine linguistic output; but his view of what mere matter might or might not do was coloured by a very crude conception of material stuff as purely geometrical extension, so there must be an element of speculation in trying to transfer his arguments to the context of our far richer contemporary physics and neurology. However that may be, it

---

34. Descartes, *Discourse on the Method*, pt. 5, AT, vol. 6, 56–57; CSM, vol. 1, 140.

is now time to take stock and ask how much, if anything, of Descartes's legacy on these matters is worth preserving. For all its problems, does the Cartesian picture of the human being as composed of a "rational soul" as well as a body have any residual lessons to teach us about our human nature?

As we have seen, Descartes had understandable worries about how our human conceptual ability, our creative power of thought and language, could possibly be realized in a finite mechanistic system. But even acknowledging the reasonableness of his concerns (especially given the knowledge then available to him about the brain and nervous system), it is hard to see how positing an incorporeal soul actually solves any explanatory puzzles. Making the principle responsible for thought immaterial as opposed to material doesn't *explain* how the putative "soul" does the job of generating the indefinitely complex and flexible responses necessary for genuine thought. Is today's physicalist approach, discarding any talk of souls and focusing instead on the structure and workings of the brain, any better off? It is true that scientists are still far from being able to explain exactly how the brain does the job of enabling us to think and reason; but cognitive science is still, relatively speaking, in its infancy, and there are very few people who now doubt that the cerebral cortex is indeed the organ responsible for thought, and that thought and reasoning occur in virtue of the electrical and chemical activity that takes place there.

That said, it cannot be denied that we human beings, in view of our capacities for genuine thought and language, are radically different from anything so far found elsewhere in the universe. To be sure, we are now much more aware than was Descartes of our continuity with the animal kingdom; but the fact remains that no animal can produce linguistic output whose complexity even comes remotely close to that found "even in the dullest of men," as Descartes puts it.[35] When we reflect further on our unique human capacities, even if we go with the flow of modern cognitive science and discard Descartes's immaterial soul, replacing it with the complex physical configuration of the brain, we cannot deny that what is involved when that physical process is activated is a whole world of *meaning*—of thoughts and reflections and understandings and willings and ponderings—that has a life and significance of its own; it cannot be reduced to, or read off from, the physical events studied by the brain scientist. So even if Descartes was mistaken in supposing it necessary to invoke an immaterial substance to explain this, it nevertheless remains true that the activities he chose to ascribe to the soul are *irreducible attributes of our human nature*—they belong to us "in their own right," as it were, and they define what it is to be human in a way that resists being subsumed under the descriptions and methods of physical science. If this is right, then in the task of understanding our human nature—a task that still confronts us today—we seem to have grounds at least for a kind of *attributive dualism*, a dualism of two inherently distinct and incommensurable kinds of property or attribute—the physical properties of the body (with its brain and nervous system) and the mental properties of thinking and understanding. We can hold on to this attributive dualism, even if we firmly reject a dualism of two distinct kinds of entity or substance (the body plus an utterly separate and distinct immaterial soul).

A rough and ready way of expressing the idea just broached would be to say that understanding our human nature requires us to follow two incommensurable and distinct paths of explanation: one that invokes the physical processes undergirding our mental activities, and one that refers to our conceptual grasp of

---

35. Descartes, *Discourse on the Method*, pt. 5, AT, vol. 6, 57; CSM, vol. 1, 140.

the meaning of those activities. The idea has received sophisticated treatment by some modern philosophers,[36] and it is also
one that has historical roots in the philosophy of Spinoza (himself greatly influenced by Descartes's distinction between the
attributes of thought and of extension), as well as having something in common with the Aristotelian "hylemorphic" approach
sketched out earlier. We can consider ourselves in material
terms, "under the attribute of extension," as Spinoza put it,
looking at the physical processes of the body and brain and nervous system; or we can consider ourselves "under the attribute
of thought," looking at our ideas and beliefs and desires, and the
whole web of concepts and meanings that constitutes our conscious human lives as thinkers.[37] We might not want today to
refer to this latter domain as the domain of the "soul," for the
connotations of that term may seem to many people too "spooky"
and immaterialist to make it acceptable. But what we cannot
deny, and what Descartes, to his credit, conspicuously succeeded
in alerting us to, is that there is a vital part of what it is to be
human that necessarily eludes the quantitative and mechanistic
categories of scientific explanation.

The Soul-Body Unit and Descartes's Trialism

We are physical, biological, beings. And we are also conscious,
thinking, concept-using beings. These two aspects of our
nature are intertwined, perhaps far more so than Descartes
supposed, but to a considerable extent they nevertheless have

36. Davidson, "Mental Events" [1970].

37. Spinoza, *Ethics*, pt. 2, prop. 21: "The Mind and the Body are one and the same
Individual, which is conceived now under the attribute of Thought, now under the
attribute of Extension."

to be understood in non-overlapping conceptual categories, neither being reducible to the other. This is the residual truth in Descartes's dualistic distinction between the category of thought and that of extension.

But the complexities of our human nature are far from exhausted by these two categories, and, perhaps unexpectedly, Descartes himself realized and indeed underlined this point. One of these complexities arises from the diverse and heterogeneous character of conscious experience. Though Descartes himself does not actually use the term "consciousness" except on rare occasions, the acts he ascribed to the "rational soul" were, as we have seen, conscious acts involving the use of concepts—acts of thinking, willing, understanding, attending, and so on, which he maintained could not be explained in physical terms. One could say, then, that Descartes held consciousness to be resistant to physical explanation. This focus of his worry here about consciousness is, however, rather different from that which typically exercises today's philosophers of mind and cognitive scientists. Nowadays, researchers are preoccupied with what is called the "hard" problem of consciousness—namely, the subjective or qualitative aspect of "what it is like" for the subject to smell a rose, for example, or to taste chocolate.[38] The problem is taken to be how we could possibly provide a physically based scientific explanation of "qualia," or qualitative sensory awareness. But Descartes's primary concern, as we have seen, is with human *thought and rationality*; it is not about subjective "qualia," but about our linguistic and conceptual abilities, which he thought could not possibly be accounted for in quantitative or mechanistic terms.

Descartes did, nevertheless, think a lot about the character of our sensory awareness. In the case of the sensation of pain, for

38. Nagel, 'What is it Like to Be a Bat?'

example, we find Descartes employing an interestingly hesi-
tant phrase, when he talks of pain as "that I know-not-what
sensation"(*iste nescio-quod doloris sensus*).[39] Descartes goes on
in the same passage to talk of hunger as a *"nescio-quae vellicatio
ventriculi"*: an "I-know-not-what tugging in the stomach." The
nescio-quae in Descartes's original Latin (like *je ne sais quelle*, in
the later French translation of the *Meditations*) conveys more
than just imprecision. What seems to be implied is that there is
something here that defies cognitive specification or objective
description, but which you have to experience, from the point
of view of a subject, to know what is being talked about. So it
seems plausible to think that in his account of the "I know-not-
what" aspect of pain, Descartes is anticipating the idea that pain
and other conscious states (such as hunger and thirst) have a distinctive and irreducible phenomenological character accessible
only to the subject. We shall return to these important aspects
of the human psyche, the dimension of opacity and the dimension of subjectivity, in subsequent chapters.[40]

Despite what labels like "Cartesian dualism" or "the ghost in
the machine" might suggest, Descartes was *not* ready to ascribe
such sensory experience straightforwardly to an immaterial soul.
On the contrary, he thought of sensations and feelings and passions and appetites as *bearing witness to our embodied nature as
creatures of flesh and blood*. There is, for Descartes, more to a
human being than a bodily machine moved around by an incorporeal soul. He emphatically dissociated his position from
Platonic-style "angelism"—the reduction of human beings to the

39. Descartes, *Meditations*, Sixth Meditation, AT, vol. 7, 76; CSM, vol. 2, 53.
40. For the subjective aspect, see ch. 3, and for the problem of opacity, ch. 4. We
shall also return to the in some ways problematic notion of "irreducibility" in ch. 5,
"Reaching Forward to the Transcendent."

status of immaterial souls making use of bodies.[41] Descartes insisted, on the contrary, that in human beings mind and body are united "in a real and substantial manner" by a "true mode of union"; and our sensations (like hunger, thirst, pleasure, and pain) bear witness to this intimate union. Speculating on what it would be like if we were purely thinking beings, like an angel, Descartes suggests that an angel would have thoughts, but would not have sensations:

> If an angel were in a human body, it would not have sensations as we do, but would simply perceive the motions which are caused by external objects, and in this way would differ from *a real human being.*[42]

Sensory experience, our vivid awareness through sight, hearing, taste, smell, and touch of the world around us, and our internal bodily awareness of a variety of pleasurable and painful sensations, is the signature of a genuine human being, an embodied creature of flesh and blood.

All this puts Descartes's "dualism" in a rather different light from the way it is normally presented. For it turns out that not two, but *three* categories are needed, according to Descartes, in order to do justice to our human nature. A strictly dualistic framework recognizes only two types of notion: the soul, or immaterial mental substance, and the body, with its physical structures and mechanisms. But when a thinking substance is joined with a body so as to form a truly integrated unit, then there arises, for Descartes, a new and distinct kind of phenomenon: sensory experience, which cannot be attributed to mind simpliciter, nor

41. Descartes, *Meditations*, Fourth Replies, AT, vol. 7, 227–28; CSM, vol. 2, 160.

42. Descartes, letter to Regius, January 1642, AT, vol. 3, 493; CSMK, 206; emphasis added. Cf. letter to More, 5 February 1649, AT, vol. 5, 270; CSMK, 361.

to the body, but which is a distinctive kind of attribute belonging to genuine human beings.[43]

In his correspondence with Princess Elizabeth of Bohemia, who had questioned him about the "substantial union" of mind and body, Descartes made it quite explicit that his account of human nature requires a threefold distinction that cannot be reduced to a simple duality. There are not two but three "primitive notions" that are "the patterns on the basis of which we form all our other conceptions": the notion of soul (comprising intellection and volition), of body (defined in terms of shape and motion), and of the union of the two (on which sensation depends):

> As regards body, we have only the notion of extension, which entails the notions of shape and motion; as regards the soul on its own, we have only the notion of thought, which includes the perceptions of the intellect and the inclinations of the will; lastly, as regards the soul and the body together, we have only the notion of their union, on which depend our notions of the soul's power to move the body, and the body's power to act on the soul and cause its sensations and passions.[44]

Descartes's conception of the mind-body union as a "primitive notion" may at first seem inconsistent with his doctrine that humans owe their existence to just two basic substances, soul and body, thinking substance and extended substance. But the "trialism" Descartes is arguing for does not mean he thinks there are three kinds of substance; rather, it is an *attributive* trialism.

---

43. Some commentators have argued that Descartes failed, in the end, to sustain a convincing theory of human nature; see Voss, "End of Anthropology."

44. Descartes, letter, 21 May 1642, AT, vol. 3, 665; CSMK, 218.

The mind-body complex that constitutes a human being is the bearer of distinctive and irreducible properties in its own right; in this sense we might say that water is a "primitive" notion, meaning that it is not a mere mixture but a genuine compound, possessing attributes "in its own right" (distinctive "watery" characteristics that cannot be reduced to the properties of either of the two fundamental elements, hydrogen and oxygen, that make it up). The upshot is that in virtue of our embodied state, as creatures of flesh and blood, human beings enjoy modes of awareness that (to use Descartes's own language) "must not be referred either to the mind alone or to the body alone."[45] This "trialistic" Cartesian model is not without its problems, but it does reveal a Descartes who offered a much richer and more nuanced picture of the human condition than might appear if we focus exclusively on his two-substance dualism.

The Ethical Implications of Human Embodiment

The significant landmarks we have been uncovering in the evolution of the concept of the soul may have a certain historical interest, but it is time to stand back and ask what significance, if any, they have for how we are to think about the human condition, and for the project of "finding the soul"—the quest to understand our true nature and how we are to live. The poet W. B. Yeats is one among the many subsequent thinkers who have been influenced by the tradition of soul-body dualism derived from Plato and indeed from Descartes (despite the complications and added nuances in the latter's position that we have just been exploring). For Yeats, a human being is, ontologically speaking, an immortal soul "fastened to a dying animal." An old

45. Descartes, *Principles*, pt. 1, art. 48.

man is a mind trapped in a decaying body, and as he grows older,

> an aged man is but a paltry thing, unless
> soul clap its hands and sing and louder sing
> for every tatter in its mortal dress.[46]

Yet how can the soul "clap its hands and sing"? For Plato, as we saw at the start of this chapter, the soul's essential activities are intellectual and rational, and its highest flourishing must consist in theoretical contemplation. This feeds through to Descartes, nearly two millennia later, with his idea of an immaterial "rational soul," and the conception, developed in his metaphysical writings, of philosophical understanding as requiring us to focus on the "clear and distinct ideas" implanted in the soul by God.[47]

But can we, should we, live like that? Clearly our rational and logical abilities are a wonderful endowment, and must play a key role in any coherent conception of human flourishing. But there is more to being human than this. As we have just seen, Descartes, for all his vaunted "dualism," had the insight that we are *not* just incorporeal souls fastened to the machine of the body, but are, as human beings, fully embodied, "intermingled" with the body, and as a result of this we enjoy a whole distinctive range of new attributes, which present problems and opportunities of their own, and which need to figure in any plausible blueprint for a good human life. In the last work he published, the *Passions of the Soul*, Descartes aimed to show how humans could come to terms with the emotions and feelings that are an inescapable part of their embodied nature.

---

46. Yeats, "Sailing to Byzantium" [1928], st. 2.
47. Descartes, *Principles*, pt. 1, art. 30.

Recognizing, as Descartes does, that our emotions belong to us not *qua* purely immaterial souls, but as embodied creatures of flesh and blood, has crucial implications for how we understand ourselves as moral beings. Some of the previous ethical systems developed by the Greeks tended to take on an intellectualist or "ratiocentric" bias, which led to problems about applying a rationally devised life plan to the awkwardly recalcitrant realm of human feeling and emotion. The Cartesian model for science seems at first to be even more ratiocentric, viewing the world as an abstract, mathematically ordered system of "extended matter in motion,"[48] and construing the human contemplators of that system as purely thinking things, detached from the world of extension, and alienated even from the physical mechanisms of their own bodies.[49] But Descartes's attempt to develop a distinctive "anthropology," a theory of the genuine embodied human being, puts all this in a rather different focus. For Descartes admits, and indeed insists, that although metaphysical reasoning reveals a rigidly dualistic world of extended matter confronted by incorporeal intellect, our own daily experience as human beings provides a very different perspective—one coloured by the intimate and urgent feeling and emotion that are characteristic of a genuine human being.

Talk of an immaterial soul might suggest that each of us is the cognitive pilot of an alien bodily machine. But the reality, as Descartes observed, is that my body is not just an instrument, but is in a special and intimate sense "mine."[50] And the rich and vivid sensory and emotional life that arises from our intimate union with the body is testimony to that. Descartes admitted that the

48. See, for example, Descartes, *Principles*, pt. 2, arts. 4, 36, 37.
49. Descartes, *Treatise on Man*, AT, vol. 11, 120; CSM, vol. 1, 99.
50. Descartes, *Meditations*, Sixth Meditation, AT, vol. 7, 76; CSM, vol. 2, 52.

way in which this happens was beyond the power of philosophical reason to explicate fully: it simply has to be grasped on the
level of our inner experience.[51] But the fact that our emotional
and sensory experience is an ineradicable part of what it is to be
human has vital importance for our self-understanding, and for
the conduct of our lives. We cannot simply understand ourselves
as purely "thinking things," abstract intellects detached from the
material world of extended mechanisms, contemplating it
and manipulating it from a distance. That is how an angel, or a
ghost, might relate to the physical world. But we humans are
in the world of matter, intimately compounded with it and "intermingled" with it. To understand what makes us most fully
and distinctively human, we cannot think just in terms of our
rational and conceptual powers, plus the purely material mechanisms of the body. In addition to these two categories we need
to focus also on a third and vitally important set of human attributes: the attributes that relate to the affective dimension that
characterizes our daily experience as creatures of flesh and
blood.[52] Understanding and coming to terms with the complexity of our emotions, and bringing them into harmony with
our rationally chosen goals and projects, are a vital part of the
healing and integration of the human psyche. We shall return to
this vital element of "finding the soul" in chapter 4.

51. "What belongs to the union of the soul and the body is known only obscurely
by the intellect . . . but it is known very clearly by the senses. . . . Metaphysical
thoughts, which exercise the pure intellect, help to familiarize us with the notion of
the soul; the study of mathematics . . . accustoms us to form very distinct notions of
body. But it is the ordinary course of life and conversation, and abstention from
meditation . . . that teaches us how to conceive the union of the soul and body": letter
to Elizabeth, 28 June 1643, AT, vol. 3, 691–92; CSMK, 227.
52. For a fuller treatment of these themes, see Cottingham, *Cartesian Reflections*,
ch. 12.

As we come to the end of this necessarily very selective look at some of the milestones in the evolution of the concept of the soul in the classical, medieval, and early-modern periods,[53] it may be worth underlining a few of the more important points that should have emerged. The first is that, going right back to Plato, the soul is associated with that rational part of us that has the ability to apprehend universal and timeless truths that transcend the empirical world of the senses. In this sense the soul, we might say, is an "instrument of transcendence."[54] Whether or not we agree with Plato that this part of us is able to survive the death of the body, the fact that we have a "soul" in this sense, that our minds are endowed with this extraordinary ability, is a vital and distinctive part of our human nature, and one that must play a crucial role in how we conceive of ourselves and how we propose to live. We shall return to the theme of transcendence in our final chapter. Second, we may take from Aristotle the powerful insight that it is not necessary to conceive of the soul as a wholly independent substance essentially distinct from matter, but that it may be thought of *attributively*, in terms of form or function—an aspect of our nature as human beings that is realized in the material structures of the body, yet which is not reducible to a purely material property. And finally from Descartes we may take some vital insights that continue to inform and enrich our present-day grasp of our human nature, and its relation to the world as disclosed by the methods of modern science. For even if we discard Descartes's inheritance, via Plato, Aristotle, and Aquinas, of an immaterial "rational soul," we can see the force of his insistence on the very special nature of our rational and conceptual powers

53. For a lucid and informative coverage of these and other milestones, see Goetz and Taliaferro, *Brief History*.

54. For this phrase, used by Thomas Nagel, see *Mind and Cosmos*, 85.

and how they defy mechanistic reduction. We can also acknowledge his insights into the strange ineffable quality of the psychophysical modes of awareness we call sensations. And we can follow him in striving to integrate our philosophical conception of ourselves as rational beings with acceptance of our embodied nature, and the resultant need to make an accommodation with the emotions or "passions of the soul" that are crucial to finding our true selves, and achieving fulfilment.

(3)

Soul, Science, and Subjectivity

> I see no contradiction in it, that the first eternal thinking
> Being should, if he pleased, give to certain systems of created
> senseless matter, put together as he thinks fit, some degrees of
> sense, perception, and thought.
>
> —JOHN LOCKE, *ESSAY CONCERNING HUMAN*
> *UNDERSTANDING*

Objective Science and Subjective Experience

By way of taking stock of where we have arrived so far, let us go back to that strange and resonant phrase of Descartes that was quoted at the end of our opening chapter: "this *me* [*ce moi*], that is to say the soul, by which I am what I am." Descartes's use of the first-person pronoun in this and many similar passages is profoundly significant. What he takes each of us to be aware of is something that is directly accessed from a first-person perspective. You can investigate me from the outside, measure my brain states, collect any other data about my body and nervous system that you please, but you cannot enter the conscious domain of which I am directly aware and which seems to give me my very sense of what it is to be myself—"this *me*, that is to say the soul, by which I am what I am." I am not an object or item to be measured through the quantitative methods of science; I am a *subject*—the owner, as it were, of the thoughts and feelings and experiences that constitute my conscious life.

Descartes, in the very next words after the phrase just quoted, went on to assert, much more controversially and problematically, that this *me* is "entirely distinct from the body and could exist without it."[1] As we saw in the previous chapter, Descartes's eventual account of my relation to my body is far more nuanced and complex than this suggests; for when I am considered not as a "rational soul" but as a *human being*, with all the sensory and emotional life that this entails, then I am on Descartes's view essentially and intimately connected with my body. But despite this recognition of our human embodiment, Descartes continued to regard the core thinking self, "this *me*, that is to say the soul, by which I am what I am," as immaterial.

Yet even if we consider the bare notion of "this me," the first-person subject of experience, there seems to be no necessary or valid argument that compels us to move from the irreducibility of this first-personal perspective to the conclusion that what is taking up this perspective must be a separate substance or entity. I am a unique subject of thought and experience; so much is granted. But a *subject* in this sense need not be a *substance*. A substance, in traditional philosophical terminology, is an independent entity that is capable of existing on its own, or in its own right.[2] But for all Descartes, or anyone else, has shown, the very being of "this me," this "soul" or subject of consciousness, could be fundamentally dependent on and bound up with the physical, biological, and neurological processes going on in the body of this particular biological creature, this human that is me.

We can combine this suggestion with the "attributive" view of the soul canvassed in the previous chapter. Granting that I am aware of myself from the first-personal perspective, as a subject

1. Descartes, *Discourse on the Method*, pt. 4.
2. Aristotle, *Categories*, ch. 5; Descartes, *Principles*, pt. 1, art. 51.

of experience, a unique "me," nevertheless this subjectivity, this "me-ness," may reasonably be understood not as a "thing," not as an independent substance, but as an *attribute* or property of this particular complex biological organism that is a member of the species *Homo sapiens.*

Consider how this might be the case. I owe my individual existence to the conjoining many years ago of a human egg and sperm, the successful fusion of gametes to form a new organism, which began to grow, first as an embryo, then as a developing foetus, until it emerged as a human baby. In some of these early stages, many of the attributes or properties I now enjoy were not present—there was, for example, no capacity for kicking until the legs were formed and the muscles and nervous system were sufficiently developed, and there was no capacity for sight until the eyes were properly formed and all the other relevant cerebral functions were acquired. These and many, many other capacities and activities are clearly not independently existing substances or entities but are *attributes* or *properties* of the biological creature as it grows and develops. And in this process of growth there will come a point, perhaps first in a rudimentary form, and then as the basics of language are gradually acquired, when this biological creature begins to develop a sense of being a "*me.*" Just as it developed the capacity for kicking or seeing, so it develops over time that sense of subjectivity, of "me-ness," of selfhood, that is so crucial to our humanity. The biological organism has become a *subject of experience.* But we do not need to say that an additional entity or substance has come into existence (or been divinely implanted into the body) when this happens. We can say instead that what emerges, once the organism with its brain and nervous system has reached a suitably complex developmental stage, is the attribute or property so distinctive of our humanity, the property of having, as it were, a subjective point of view.

Something could presumably be conscious without being a subject in the rich sense just described. Indeed, it seems we have all been through such a stage as babies, though we cannot remember or properly conceive of it. What about non-human animals? It is natural in many contexts to attribute conscious states to them (sensory and perceptual states, for example), and the greater the complexity of these, the more it becomes reasonable to think that they too are subjects of experience. Some of the mammals even appear to have a more or less developed sense of self, though the extent of this is disputed.[3] But without going into the notoriously difficult terrain of the differences between human and animal experience, it may confidently be said that no animal could formulate the Cartesian idea of "this *me* by which I am what I am." Questions about the kinds and degrees of consciousness are a matter for heated debate among philosophers and scientists. But none of these debates should in any way cast doubt on the reality of the mental life that each of us human beings enjoys as a subject, as a "me." Nor can they undermine the highly plausible and widely accepted notion that this subjectivity, this "me-ness" belongs to, and is dependent on the physical functioning of, this particular biological creature (in my case, the particular human being who is now writing these words).

Plausible though this notion may be, problems and puzzles remain. When we think about the relationship between our mental lives and the physical world of which we are a part, we seem to be pulled in opposite directions. On the one hand (in the light of all that has been and is being discovered about the

3. See Gallup, "Self-Awareness in Primates."

workings of the brain) we want to say that if we could somehow specify all the relevant brain states of a living human animal, all the hugely complex electrochemical and other parameters, then this must be sufficient for human consciousness. So if, so to speak, one were God, and wanted to create a thinking, self-conscious being like you or me, then all one would have to do would be to create a biological creature with the right kind of cerebral complexity. The biological states and properties, suitably activated, must surely in themselves be enough to do the job. But on the other hand—and here we seem to be pulled in the opposite direction—there appears to be a curious gap between the objectively describable physical properties and the conscious lifeworld of the individual subject. How do we get from the objective physical configurations of the brain and body, as investigated by science, to the unique subjective centre of consciousness that is me, or you?

Here the "scientistic" doctrine that there is no truth or reality that cannot in principle be accommodated via the methods and language of physical science, seems to run into a major obstacle. As Descartes put it, when he made his fundamental distinction between the domain of *res extensa* (whatever is studied by quantitative physics) and the domain of *res cogitans*, conscious thought, "there is nothing in body, nothing the extended world, that savours of thought."[4] If we start with physics, from the fundamental laws at the top, down to the minutest specifications of particular physical states and processes, it seems that we cannot derive from any of this the unique point of view of the individual thinker—this *me* by which I am what I am.

4. "*Nihil quod redoleat cogitationem*": Descartes, *Meditations*, Fourth Replies, AT, vol. 7, 227; CSM, vol. 2, 160.

Consciousness: Illusion or Irreducible Reality?

The phenomenon of subjectivity generates a whole cluster of philosophical puzzles. For example, the philosopher Stephen Priest, following in the footsteps of Thomas Nagel, has been much exercised by the disturbing question young children sometimes ask—"Why am I me?" or "What is it that makes me *me*?" Suppose (to follow up the nightmare scenario from Aldous Huxley's *Brave New World*) that the room is full of my identical twins, all having identical thoughts about some philosophical topic. Even if, *per impossibile*, we could consult the unimaginably complicated "printout" of the cerebral states and activities of each individual,[5] we could still not derive the information that will determine which one of those people is *me*. There's only one way of knowing you are *you*, and that is to *be* the conscious subject that is you, and to experience this subjectivity "from the inside," as it were.[6]

Are these puzzles confusions—a case of philosophers raising the dust and then complaining they cannot see (in George Berkeley's phrase, though it might equally have been penned by Wittgenstein)?[7] In one way, to be sure, it seems to be no more than a tautological truth that one cannot get from the impersonal view from nowhere to the personal view from somewhere. So

5. Since the human brain is almost infinite in its complexity, to produce a "connectome" mapping out all the neural pathways of the brain, with its over 85 billion neurons and 100 trillion synapses, remains far outside the realm of practical possibility (though work on the connectome of the vastly simpler worm *Caenorhabditis elegans*—302 neurons and 7000 synapses—has begun). See Chen "In Lofty Quest."

6. Priest, "Radical Internalism"; Nagel, *View from Nowhere*.

7. Berkeley, *Principles of Human Knowledge*, introduction, sec. 3. Cf. Wittgenstein, *Philosophical Investigations*, pt. 1, sec. 309: "What is your aim in philosophy? To show the fly the way out of the fly-bottle."

we need to be careful about how we understand the pronounce-
ment made by Roger Scruton in a recent book on human nature, that "the subject is in principle unobservable to science,"
or that it is "not part of the empirical world."[8] For the fact that
the objective, impersonal language of science doesn't encompass
the perspective of the conscious subject doesn't at all show that
what is *having* the experience is not the self-same biological and
physical object described by science. Here the contemporary
philosophical consensus, which seems pretty much unassailable,
is that the dualistic inference drawn by Descartes, assigning
thinking subjects to a separate ontological realm, was misguided.
Conscious subjects (at least those we know of on Earth) are not
incorporeal substances but *human beings*, specimens of the species *Homo sapiens*, biological creatures of flesh and blood.

And yet it is now that the really interesting problem begins.
Let us agree that consciousness is a property of a physical, biological creature, a human being. The fundamental problem is
how we are to fit *that* property of human beings into a coherent
conception of reality as a whole—to fit it into our world view,
if you like. The British philosopher Tim Crane has recently observed, "we know with as much certainty as we know anything
that we have conscious thoughts and experiences." And this
psychological reality, Crane goes on to argue, is *irreducible*. For
the very project in which so many cognitive scientists are now
engaged, of correlating conscious experience with neural
activity—with bits of the brain lighting up, and all the rest—
could not even get under way without presupposing that consciousness is real, "as real as the neural activity with which it is
correlated."[9]

8. Scruton, *Human Nature*, 32.
9. Crane, "How We Can Be," 8.

Yet, remarkably, by no means all of those who have reflected on this topic are prepared to concede that consciousness is real. Or at least, they refuse to concede that it is real in what they implicitly take to be the only truly authentic sense—that applying to the phenomena studied by science. In his book *Soul Dust* the biologist Nicholas Humphrey argues that conscious awareness is a kind of *illusion* created by the brain, or a part of the brain. It is an internal "magical mystery show" that evolved because of its survival value—roughly because it makes life more enjoyable and motivates people to continue wanting to live.[10] In somewhat similar vein, Daniel Dennett, in his book *From Bacteria to Bach and Back*, has called consciousness a "user-illusion." It is comparable to:

> the ingenious user-illusion of click-and-drag icons, little tan folders into which files may be dropped, and the rest of the ever more familiar items on your computer's desktop. What is actually going on behind the desktop is mind-numbingly complicated, but users don't need to know about it, so intelligent interface designers have simplified the affordances, making them particularly salient for human eyes, and adding sound effects to help direct attention. Nothing compact and salient inside the computer corresponds to that little tan file-folder on the desktop screen.[11]

In other words, a clever designer has made something "salient" for us computer users, to help us do certain things, but *there's nothing really there* in the computer that directly corresponds to the visible properties of the desktop icon: it's all an illusion, though a very useful one. And similarly in the human case

10. Humphrey, *Soul Dust*, 49–50.
11. Dennett, *From Bacteria to Bach and Back*, 198.

(though of course Dennett is not suggesting that there is any designer, just the blind, random process of evolution), we have
evolved to have brains of mind-numbing complexity that enable
us to navigate around the world, survive, perform a host of complex operations, but the subjective qualitative awareness we
have of the world doesn't point to anything real—all that's really
going on are the physical processes that make up our environment plus the extraordinarily complicated brain processes inside
our head; *this is all the reality there is.*

Such privileging of the abstract scientific picture of reality (expressed in quantitative, mathematical, and mechanical terms)
over the "manifest image" presented to conscious awareness has
an old philosophical history.[12] But the downgrading of the manifest image as less real is a confusion, or at all events philosophically quite unwarranted. Even a philosopher as brilliant as Bertrand Russell was once tempted to say—absurdly—that tables
and chairs are not "really" solid, on the spurious grounds that
they are made up of atoms that largely consist of gaps (the empty
space between protons and electrons).[13] The truth, of course, is
that the table I write on is really and genuinely solid; this is quite
compatible with its being composed of arrangements of atoms

12. See, for example, Nicolas Malebranche's vigorous attack in *La recherche de la
vérité*, first published in 1674, on the "error" whereby almost everyone believes that
"heat is in the fire . . . and colours in coloured objects" (*Search after Truth*, bk. 1,
ch. 11), and Locke's assault on the "vulgar" way of talking "as if Light and Heat were
really something in the Fire more than a power to excite [certain] Ideas in us" (*Essay
concerning Human Understanding*, bk. 2, ch. 31, § 2). For a discussion of Descartes's
views, which influenced both these thinkers, see Cottingham, *Cartesian Reflections*,
ch. 7. The contrast between the "manifest image" (arising from our ordinary lived
experience of the world) and the "scientific image" was drawn by Wilfred Sellars in
1956, in *Empiricism*.

13. Russell, *Problems of Philosophy*, ch. 1.

that are not themselves solid. *Both* the ordinary macro-properties manifest to consciousness *and* the scientifically discovered micro-properties are perfectly genuine, and it is a philosophical mistake to privilege either by saying one is more "real" than the other.

To revert to Dennett's analogy, when I see the icon on my computer desktop, there is nothing illusory about it (it would only be an illusion if, for example, I had never seen a computer before, and tried to peel off the folder as if it were stuck on to the front of the glass screen). The technology behind the icon may be a marvel of science, but when the image of the folder appears on my computer desktop I see it quite clearly and understand perfectly well what it signifies, since I understand it *conceptually* as representing a location where information is stored, something that has a *meaning* for me, a meaning that is related by analogy to the function of a paper folder where I can keep photographs or offprints. That conceptual understanding operates relative to a whole network of other concepts that make up my picture of who I am, how I relate to the world and to other human beings, and what my plans and purposes are. That complex semantic lifeworld is *irreducible*: it may require to be underpinned by mechanisms that are ultimately physical—Dennett may be right about that, and Descartes may have turned out to be wrong about the limitations of physical brains, and of matter generally. But what Descartes was *not* wrong about was the irreducible reality of conscious thought and of the rich conceptually mediated lifeworld to which each of us has access as a conscious subject of experience.[14]

14. I shall return to the in some ways problematic notion of "irreducibility" in ch. 5, "Natural versus Supernatural."

The Panpsychist Turn

At the opposite end of the spectrum from those who attempt to deny or downgrade the reality of consciousness are those who grant that it is indeed an authentic and irreducible aspect of reality, but who propose to construe it as somehow fundamental to the nature of the physical world. This kind of outlook has come to be known as "panpsychism," meaning, as the Greek root *psyche* suggests, that all of physical reality is fundamentally "soul-like," or, more prosaically, that mental properties are somehow fundamental to the nature of the universe.

An interesting feature of such views is how far they run against the tide of Darwinian thinking that has shaped so much of the modern outlook. For the assumption of the Darwinian approach is that consciousness is evolutionarily speaking a latecomer on the scene. For billions of years there is no consciousness, just dead, unthinking matter, swirling around and exploding and coalescing, forming galaxies and suns. And then some suns explode and produce heavier elements. And then planets form. And then on some of those planets, or at least the one that we know of, life emerges from non-living matter, and then, after millennia of complexification, consciousness at last emerges, as a kind of by-product. In the words of Stephen Hawking, the human race is "just a chemical scum on a moderate-sized planet, orbiting around a very average star in the outer suburb of one among a hundred billion galaxies."[15] On the panpsychist picture, by contrast, consciousness is somehow intrinsically part of the nature of things from the very start.

---

15. Stephen Hawking, from an interview with Ken Campbell on the British TV series for Channel 4, *Reality on the Rocks: Beyond Our Ken*, aired 26 February 1995.

Panpsychists tend to accept the typical modern secularist consensus that the only fundamental entities in the universe are physical entities, but propose that there is *more to the nature of those entities than the physical sciences make known to us*. In addition to what the physical sciences make known—namely, the causal structures and dispositions characterizable ultimately in the language of mathematical physics—it is proposed that all matter has the irreducible intrinsic property of consciousness. In line with suggestions made by Bertrand Russell and Arthur Eddington in the 1920s, the deep nature of the material world might (albeit in a way that is hidden from us) somehow explain mentality.[16]

If this means, as some panpsychists propose, that every tiny particle or portion of matter is somehow "proto-experiential," or contains the germ of consciousness, then it faces the "combination" problem first raised by William James: even if we can grasp the idea that reality is composed of millions of tiny subjects of experience, we are no nearer understanding how they could combine to form a "large-scale" conscious subject like you or me.[17] In general, looking for consciousness at the micro level seems to be a kind of category mistake, since perception, thought, understanding, and so on look very much like holistic or "large-scale" properties, properties that are ascribable to persons rather than particles.

A version of panpsychism that takes the "large-scale" nature of consciousness seriously is the *cosmopsychism* proposed by the English philosopher Philip Goff. On this view, the cosmos in its deep nature is constituted by a kind of expansive cosmic

16. Russell, *Analysis of Matter*; Eddington, *Physical World*. Discussed in Goff, *Consciousness and Fundamental Reality*, ch. 6.

17. James, *Principles of Psychology*, 160.

consciousness, which "enfolds" all things into a single unified nature.[18] This begins now to sound as if it has points of contact with a traditional theistic outlook; but Goff, like the majority of contemporary philosophers, is unwilling to depart from a broadly naturalist or physicalist world view. He regards the cosmos as a material entity, along with the conscious subjects that inhabit it, and holds that physical science, as far as it goes, offers a perfectly valid description of its causal structure, even though it cannot tell us about its intrinsic nature. The consciousness that is supposed to be intrinsic to matter thus turns out on this view to be a *transcendent* property, at least in the sense that it transcends the boundaries of science—there is no conceivable scientific experiment, observation, or test that could detect it.

Now the notion of there being limits to the scope of science should not in itself be problematic: we have already had occasion to note that there are serious problems with the "scientistic" doctrine that science is the measure of all reality and truth;[19] and we have drawn attention to the fact that our conscious human lifeworld, woven out of our thoughts and feelings and emotions, is irreducible in the sense that it cannot be captured or fully explained in scientific terms. Yet once we have got as far as recognizing the irreducible and intractable (in scientific terms) nature of consciousness, might it not be worth at least considering an alternative to construing it as a mysterious intrinsic property of matter—an alternative that one might suppose is staring us in the face given that it has been around for a very long time indeed? If consciousness is indeed an *irreducible aspect of reality*,

18. Goff, *Consciousness and Fundamental Reality*, 230.
19. See above, "Objective Science and Subjective Experience," and ch. 1, "But Why the Soul?"

then might not something like a traditional theistic world view offer a more hospitable framework for making sense of this remarkable fact? If we set our face against considering this option, the only remaining alternative seems the "mysterian" one of regarding consciousness as an intractable mystery: a brute fact we cannot deny but which we cannot ever hope to incorporate into any wider picture of reality.[20]

Theism, to be sure, does not claim to eliminate the mysteriousness of things, and many of the most influential Christian theologians, including Augustine and Aquinas, maintain that God is "incomprehensible"—God can never be encompassed or fully grasped by the finite human mind.[21] Nevertheless, it is a fundamental theistic belief, following the words of Genesis, that human beings are made "in the image" of God;[22] and this is taken to be especially true in virtue of our conscious minds, in virtue of our attributes of intellect and will. Theism thus posits a source or ground of all being that is somehow *mind-like*: consciousness is taken to be at the heart of reality. The theistic picture tends to be discarded or ignored by the majority of contemporary philosophers, but it seems perverse to dismiss it from consideration should it turn out to fit rather well with certain aspects of reality that cannot in integrity be denied. And it appears, from what has been said so far, that it is at least no worse equipped to accommodate the irreducible reality of consciousness than either the expedient of downgrading it as somehow illusory, or the panpsychist expedient of construing it as a mysterious intrinsic property of the physical world. This, to be

20. For "mysterianism," see McGinn, *Mysterious Flame.*
21. Augustine, *Sermons*, Sermon 52, para. 16, and Sermon 117, para. 5; Aquinas, *Summa theologiae*, pt. 1, qu. 12, art. 7.
22. Genesis 1:27.

sure, is a very modest conclusion; but perhaps from here we may be able to discern more positive reasons to favour a theistic model.

Finding a Place for Consciousness

To summarize where we have arrived so far: if consciousness is indeed a fundamental and irreducible aspect of reality, and this constitutes a prima facie problem for today's secularist materialist consensus, then should that not open the door to acknowledging at least the possibility of a theistic alternative? It may be helpful here to consider an analogous phenomenon that philosophers have struggled to fit into the materialist consensus—namely, that of *strong normativity*. By strong normativity I mean the fact that moral values and obligations exert an authoritative demand on us, whether we like it or not. We may often turn away from what is good and right, but even as we do turn away we recognize that moral demands retain an undeniable authority over us. To use an image borrowed from Gottlob Frege in the very different context of logic and mathematics, they are like boundary stones that our thought can overflow but not dislodge.[23]

Now it is extremely hard to accommodate the notion of an objective, authoritative moral requirement within an exclusively scientifically based picture of reality. One reaction to this from scientistically minded philosophers (those who acknowledge no ultimate reality outside the boundaries of science) is simply to deny the reality of such moral demands. Just as we saw in the case of consciousness, with the attempts to dismiss it as somehow illusory, so too in the case of morality, there are various

23. Frege, *Basic Laws of Arithmetic*, 13.

eliminativist or deflationary accounts that try to deny the reality of authoritative reasons for action. Thus the "projectivists" maintain that there really are no authoritative values, just our own preferences and desires.[24] Then there are the deflationary accounts of the naturalists, starting with Charles Darwin himself in the *Descent of Man*, who speaks scathingly of the "so-called moral sense," meaning that the deliverances of conscience do not provide any insight into an objective authoritative realm of values, but are reducible to one or more natural inclinations and dispositions that have developed under selection pressure.[25] Or again there is the reductionism of Sigmund Freud, who attempts to dismiss our sense of right and wrong as the harsh voice of the Superego, which owes its specious authority to the child's having unconsciously internalized the controlling voice of the parent.[26] Though there may be interesting insights to be gained along the way from these various approaches, none of them can fully explain the enduring power of our moral intuitions—the deep sense that cruelty is genuinely wrong and impermissible, or that we are required to do our best to help those in distress. There remains something about such normative requirements that cannot be reduced to mere inclination, or historically evolved propensity, or inculcated taboo. And this has led an increasing number of moral philosophers to move away from reductionist accounts towards some form of strong moral objectivism.

But if there are objective moral truths, how are they to be accommodated within the modern secular world view? Moral philosophers have wrestled with this conundrum in a way that seems in many ways to parallel the struggles of the philosophers

24. Blackburn, *Essays in Quasi-Realism.*
25. Darwin, *Descent of Man,* ch. 4, 143.
26. Freud, *New Lectures on Psychoanalysis.*

of mind over consciousness. Thus, paralleling the panpsychist suggestion of consciousness as a pervasive feature of reality, the moral philosopher Russ Shafer-Landau maintains that values are "a brute fact about the way the world works"; or, in a later formulation, "moral principles are as much a part of reality as . . . the basic principles of physics."[27] Yet against the background of the materialist-secularist consensus, this makes normative value very much a cosmic anomaly.[28] To put it very crudely, are we supposed to think that values somehow float around, alongside planets and stars and galaxies and molecules—that they just "waft by," as Christine Korsgaard has put it?[29] It is one thing to say values exist, but *how* do they exist? Similar problems beset the formulations of other realists like Eric Wielenberg, who asserts that moral truths are "part of the furniture of the universe," and indeed constitute the "ethical background of every possible universe."[30]

One of the best known modern moral objectivists, Derek Parfit, maintains, in line with the title of his mammoth last book, *On What Matters*, that some things really objectively *matter*. How we treat people really matters; whether we look after our planet so that humanity survives really matters. These are genuine moral truths. As Parfit puts it, "In believing that some things matter, I am believing that there are some *irreducibly normative truths*."[31] In other words, such moral truths have objective authority over us and give us decisive reasons to act in certain ways. But what grounds this objectivity? What makes the truths true? The

---

27. See Shafer-Landau, *Moral Realism*, 46, 48, and *Ethical Theory*, ch. 8.
28. See Mulgan, *Purpose in the Universe*, 34.
29. Korsgaard, *Sources of Normativity*, 44.
30. Wielenberg, *Value and Virtue*, 52.
31. Parfit, *On What Matters*, vol. 2, 464, emphasis added.

theistic answer would of course be that there is an objective moral order, grounded ultimately in the nature of God, independent of our mere contingent inclinations and desires, and that this order exerts a normative power or authority over us, providing us with conclusive and compelling reasons to behave in certain ways. But like many contemporary philosophers, Parfit rejects the theistic answer: he cannot accept God as the reality underlying the objective moral order. And indeed he buys into the standard materialist-naturalist paradigm: only the natural world exists, or, as he puts it, there are no "strange" parts of reality.[32] So what grounds the objective truths of morality? The perhaps amazing answer that Parfit offers is: *nothing*. Although he insists they are true, "as true as any truth could be," he holds that there is no underlying reality that makes them true: they have "*no* ontological status." According to his view, "for such claims to be true, the reason-involving properties need not exist either as natural properties in the spatio-temporal world, or in some non-spatio temporal part of reality."[33] We are left with the deeply puzzling assertion that there are ultimate moral truths that have authority over how we should live, but which are simply *true*, true without there being any truth-makers, yet "as true as any truth could be." Like so many contemporary secularist moral philosophers, Parfit wants to retain the intuition that there are compelling authoritative moral reasons, but he wants this intuition somehow to just be *true*, in a Godless and wholly material universe, without further explanation. This resort to irreducible normative truths without any truth-makers seems evidence of just how tight a grip the materialist atheist paradigm has in our philosophical culture.

32. Parfit, *On What Matters*, 487.
33. Parfit, *On What Matters*, 486.

Normativity, like consciousness, is something we are stuck with: we cannot wish it away as an illusion, and we cannot easily fit it into a purely physical picture of reality. A possible recourse at this stage might be some form of Platonism, such as that championed in modern times by Iris Murdoch, who rejects traditional theism, but puts "the Good" in place of a personal God: "Good represents the reality of which God is the dream."[34] A long-standing problem with Platonic metaphysics, never perhaps fully addressed by Murdoch, is that of explaining the ontological status of abstract forms such as "the Good"—in what sense are they supposed to be "real"? But even if that worry can be dealt with, it is hard to see how something as inert, impersonal, and abstract as a Platonic form could generate normative requirements merely by its being there to be contemplated. Murdoch here remarks that "of course Plato did not think that morality consisted in staring at an abstract idea," and goes on to speak of the need for "an orientation of our energy and appetites," through the power of love.[35] So the Good in whose reality she believes is not after all an inert form or concept, but a real power, exerting a kind of "magnetic" force (to use an analogy she frequently deploys), which, in quasi-religious fashion, can "purify our desires" and be "inescapably active in our lives."[36] There is no space here to delve deeper into Murdoch's complex and subtle position. But although she rejects the idea of a personal God, it seems that the implications of her position come very close to those of theism, notably in her insistence that we "experience the reality of the good" as "a discovery of something

34. Murdoch, *Metaphysics*, 496.
35. Murdoch, *Metaphysics*, 497.
36. Murdoch, *Metaphysics*, 109.

independent of us,"[37] something which imposes normative requirements and has transformative power.[38]

At all events, if we *are* prepared to open the door to the possibility of theism, then what looked like intractable problems—the problem of normativity, and the problem of consciousness—suddenly look more manageable. They cease to be cosmic anomalies, and start to fit into a wider picture. For with respect to normativity, the domain within which the idea of authoritative reasons for action seems naturally at home is the *personal* domain—the domain of a mind or minds endowed with and responsive to reason. And similarly, with respect to consciousness, the *personal* domain seems the only plausible domain within which we can make sense of the idea of a conscious perspective, a subjective lifeworld. God, for the theist, is the supreme personal presence, the archetypal subject who is the source of being and goodness, who enfolds and sustains all conscious thought. As Descartes observed, the individual *Cogito* ("I am thinking") is a tiny, temporary, flickering flame, ever on the brink of extinction were there not a sustaining power to preserve it.[39] On the theistic picture, God is the primordial subject who *enfolds* all that exists, without whom there would be no enduring conscious subjects, and no genuine authoritative value to guide their lives.

Some may be concerned that such a proposal involves jettisoning the scientific framework whose methods have proved their worth in countless areas of human life and knowledge. But

37. Murdoch, *Metaphysics*, 508.
38. See below, ch. 5, "Transcendence and Our Human Destiny."
39. Descartes, *Meditations*, Second Meditation, AT, vol. 7, 27 and 49; CSM, vol. 2, 15 and 43.

there is nothing in the theistic picture to contradict the findings of modern science, nothing that denies that the structure of the universe can be analysed and its workings predicted with impressive accuracy using the quantitative formulae and all the other models and mechanisms of the modern physical sciences. Nor (except for fundamentalists and scriptural literalists) does the theistic outlook clash with the idea of the universe developing over vast stretches of time, and eventually giving rise to planets, and to our own planet with its rich variety of biological forms, including ourselves. All these aspects of the scientific account remain in place. But the scientific account does not in itself encompass the very special nature of the properties we enjoy in virtue of having such complex brains and nervous systems—the attributes whereby we have conscious awareness of ourselves and the world around us, and have the power to feel and think and reflect on that awareness, and thereby to enter and be responsive to the whole domain of value and meaning. These extraordinary human powers, on the theistic picture, are not a strange cosmic anomaly but depend on our minds being, albeit in a limited and finite manner, reflections of the divine intelligence, the *logos* that enfolds all things. From the subjective horizon of our own conscious awareness, each of us looks out into a cosmos that even from our limited grasp of it we can recognize to be *intelligible*—not an arbitrary series of properties and events, but an intelligible whole, understood and held in awareness by the primordial divine mind.

The Domain of the Soul

To reflect further on the implications of the theistic view just sketched, let us return for a moment to the strange and paradoxical suggestion of Nicholas Humphrey mentioned earlier—the suggestion that consciousness is an "illusion." The latter term sounds a disparaging or dismissive one. But to his credit, Humphrey ends up acknowledging that if consciousness is in a certain sense an illusion, it is one that is of vital importance to our human lives. For in virtue of being subjects of experience, we humans live in what Humphrey calls *soul land*:

> Soul land is a territory of the spirit. It is a place where the magical interiority of human minds makes itself felt on every side. A place where you naturally assume that every other human being lives, as you do, in the extended present of phenomenal consciousness. Where you acknowledge and honour the personhood of others, treating everyone as an independent . . . responsible . . . conscious being in his or her own right. . . . It is a place where the claims of the spirit begin to rank as highly as the claims of the flesh. Where you join hands with others in sharing . . . the beauties of the world you have enchanted. . . . This spiritual territory is not only where almost all humans do live but where they *give of their best*.[40]

The glowing encomium to the wonders of "soul land" takes us back to many of the aspects of human experience that we touched on in chapter 1. We noted that the term "soul," as it occurs in novels and poetry and drama and in religious and spiritual writings, tends to be used in connection with certain central and deeply significant goals of human life—our quest to find our true "self" or identity, our search to lead integrated and morally worthwhile lives, our yearning for the affection that can give meaning to our existence, and our longing for the strange exaltation that arises from loving union with another human being or a sense of intimate harmony with the natural world. All

40. Humphrey, *Soul Dust*, 193–94, emphasis added.

these precious elements of our human birthright seem connected with the wondrous domain of "soul land"—the domain we are able to enter in virtue of what Humphrey terms "phenomenal consciousness": the bright flame of conscious awareness with which each of us is endowed.

And yet—and this is where, despite his eloquence, his argument seems to go so curiously astray—Humphrey insists that this magical mystery show is *created by us*. It is *we*, he says, who have enchanted the world. But why are *we* regarded as the creators of the magical show? Why are all the wondrous properties mentioned not fully real, but an illusion generated by us? Here once more we find the recurrent doctrinaire privileging of the scientific image over the manifest image.[41] Science has (supposedly) taught us that the only truly real properties are those expressible in the neutral, quantitatively based terminology of physics and the other natural sciences. So all the wondrous properties glowingly listed by Humphrey cannot, he thinks, be real, but must have been magicked into existence by the mind: "It was something to live in an enchanted world. But now the canopy has been lifted to reveal who is pulling the levers: it is *you*."[42]

Yet it is impossible to believe, as Humphrey would have us believe, that all this is just something *we* create. All the wonders that Humphrey, rightly, adverts to are not just smoke and mirrors, a piece of weird magic that somehow emerged as an evolutionary accident, or because it turned out to be somehow advantageous in the struggle for survival. On the contrary, the values and beauties and duties, knowledge of which we gain access to as conscious beings, are *objective* values and requirements that command our respect. We do not create them, we do

41. See note 12, above.
42. Humphrey, *Soul Dust*, 168.

not magic them into existence, we *respond* to them. The more we think about this, the more Humphrey's idea that it is *we* who call these things into existence feels all wrong. For the phenomenology—the way it feels to the subject—is not that of fantasizing or dreaming up or imagining, or of spinning a magical web: it is the phenomenology of *response*, of being confronted by, and often overwhelmed by, something wondrous, something greater than ourselves, that demands an answer from us. We are daily made aware that we are not in sole charge, not deciding by creative fiat what is valuable or what to call important. We are *confronted*—and that does not just mean impinged upon by a meaningless bombardment of particles. As the poet Rainer Maria Rilke powerfully expresses it in a famous sonnet about the compelling beauty of a statue of Apollo,[43] there are decisive moments in human experience when we are confronted by something that seems to scrutinize and find us wanting: we are called upon to change, to become something better or to "give of our best," as Humphrey himself, with commendable honesty, acknowledges. We are called on to embark on the task of "finding the soul," finding our true selves and realizing the best that we can become.

The fact that we biological creatures have these wondrous powers of conscious awareness, and these powerful moral and spiritual impulses—in short, that we manifest all the characteristics traditionally described in terms of having a "soul"—does not have to be understood as a strange purely internal or subjective phenomenon, a "magical interiority" in Humphrey's phrase. Nor does it have to be relegated to a special category of the illusory, or regarded as a bizarre cosmic anomaly. For on the theistic world view, at the heart of reality is a conscious presence,

43. Rilke, *Archaïscher Torso Apollos*, in *Neue Gedichte* [1908], pt. 2, 143–44.

the presence of the divine primordial "I" or soul in whose reality we dimly and very partially partake. This idea was given remarkable, if unorthodox, expression by Baruch Spinoza over three centuries ago, when he argued that for every physical event or configuration, there is also a conscious configuration—an idea or thought in the infinite consciousness of God.[44] So when we enter "soul land," in virtue of being conscious subjects of experience, one might say that our souls make contact, albeit in a limited and imperfect way, with the totality that is the enfolding consciousness of God.

But why bring in the divine mind? Nothing, to be sure, can compel us to do so. But once we have given up the prejudice that only the scientific image of the world corresponds to what is real, once we acknowledge the reality of what is disclosed in the "manifest image," the whole rich presence of the world around us—

> the light of setting suns,
> And the round ocean and the living air,
> And the blue sky . . . the meadows and the woods
> And mountains and . . . all that we behold
> From this green earth . . .[45]

—once we acknowledge all this, then we need to ask what the existence of this reality amounts to. A well-known wood engraving, known as the "Flammarion image" (see figure 3.1) and possibly dating from the early-modern period, shows an astronomer breaking out of the sphere of "appearances" (trees, fields, flowers, clouds, sun) and sticking his head through into the "real" world of geometrical cogs and wheels (the world disclosed by

---

44. Spinoza, *Ethics*, pt. 2, prop. 7. Citing this richly suggestive Spinozan thesis is not meant to imply wholesale agreement with his metaphysical world view.

45. Wordsworth, "Tintern Abbey," lines 98–106.

FIGURE 3.1. The "Flammarion image," from Camille Flammarion's *L'atmosphère: météorologie populaire* (Paris, [1887]); the original artist and date are unknown.

mathematical physics). It is a picture that has held many in its grip. But the quantitative descriptions of mathematical physics and mechanics are abstractions from the real lifeworld we experience. They give us theoretical models (of wonderful predictive power, to be sure) that tell us how things behave, but all such models, and indeed all science, like all human discourse, has to start from our ordinary awareness of the world around us. This lifeworld we experience and inhabit is accessed, by each of us, from the first-person perspective: it is the "phenomenal" lifeworld that Humphrey mistakenly, if in some respects understandably, characterizes as a "magical mystery show." For the world presented to consciousness is as real as can be—not a mere shadow or by-product or "epiphenomenon" or magic show, but the very touchstone of truth: anyone who denies it, or tells us that some other world (of mathematical entities, or particle interactions, or spirits, or anything else) is "more real" than the lifeworld of which I and you have immediate awareness, is denying the fundamentally *present* reality that is the basis on which any philosophical or scientific theorizing must ultimately be built.

In his "Ribblesdale," a sonnet about the overwhelming beauty of one of the Yorkshire Dales, the poet Gerard Manley Hopkins suggests that without humankind to witness and praise that beauty, nature is mute: it cannot speak but can only *be*:

> Earth, sweet Earth, sweet landscape, with leavès throng
> And louchèd low grass, heaven that dost appeal
> To, with no tongue to plead, no heart to feel
> That canst but only *be* . . .

And, in the sestet that concludes the poem, we see the role of humankind in bringing all this to conscious awareness:

> And what is Earth's eye, tongue or heart else, where
> Else, but in dear and dogged man?[46]

Human beings have a special role here, to bring the beauties of the hill and valley to life, as it were, by praising them, by giving conscious witness to the wonders spread out before them. But this does not mean that they are creating that reality, or that its existence depends on us or our minds. The poem implicitly presupposes that *of course* Ribblesdale would continue to be there, with all its beauties, its leaves and grasses and winding river, if there were no people around. The lovely dale does exist, and exists splendidly, as Hopkins goes on to say in the lines immediately following the opening section quoted above: "Thou canst but be, but that thou *well* dost." Humanity may bring these beauties to notice through consciousness, and may give voice to their wonder by praising them, but in so doing we are not creating

---

46. Hopkins, "Ribblesdale" [1882], in *Poems and Prose*, 51, emphasis added.

that reality but singing a hymn of praise to a reality that is there already.

Yet the idea of a world that is "there already," the idea of reality "in itself," independent of our (or any other creature's) ways of perceiving or conceiving of it, has puzzled and perplexed philosophers ever since Berkeley and Kant wrestled with it in the eighteenth century.[47] It seems, as the British philosopher Michael Dummett has put it, that "we can make no clear sense of there *being* a world that is not apprehended by any mind."[48] It is sometimes supposed that the world "as it is" would simply be the vast and immensely intricate physical structure of mathematically characterizable properties. But what would it be for such a complex actually to *exist*, except in the abstract and formal sense in which mathematical structures exist?[49] We seem no nearer to understanding what it could mean for something to "be there," to be "present," in itself, independently of any mental conception or conscious perception.

So what will happen when you and I are no more, or, more sombrely, when the very last human being expires (together with any other such beings there may be elsewhere in the universe)? What happens when the world is no longer "present" to me or to anyone else? Will it now be a blank, silent, dark world, a world without "presence"? Those who consider the conscious lifeworld to be a subjective illusion or magic show will presumably have to think of it this way. As the American philosopher Mark Johnston graphically describes this position:

> On the standard view of the relation between consciousness and reality, most of being is absolutely wasted, for only an

47. Berkeley, *Principles of Human Knowledge*; Kant, *Critique of Pure Reason*.
48. Dummett, *Thought and Reality*, 101.
49. Dummett, *Thought and Reality*, 98.

infinitesimally small fraction of what exists is ever *present*, that is, ever discloses or reveals some aspect of its nature. On this view, when the last individual consciousness ceases to be, the very local phenomenon of *presence* will end. The lights will have gone out, all over the universe, never to go on again.[50]

It seems deeply paradoxical and counterintuitive to suppose that the cosmos depends on us in this way in order to be actually present. But on a theistic world view, a view in which the impersonal material structures and forces of the universe are not the whole story but there is a transcendent personal consciousness at the heart of reality, "presence" is no longer produced or magicked up merely by me or you; it is no longer dependent on the puny flickering of your or my consciousness. In place of the strange, blank picture of reality as "wasted" once the "lights go out" and the last conscious subject expires, now instead we have a picture of the world, as long as it endures, as always remaining *present*, objectively *there*, understood and held in being by the universal sustaining mind of God.

Once we have made the necessary philosophical move of acknowledging the reality of the lifeworld presented to us as conscious subjects, then in integrity we have to try to fit this into an overall world picture that allows for such a reality. And since we cannot suppose that this world is created by us, and if, furthermore, we cannot see how it could be derived from the principles of physics, nor how it could be an inscrutable and unknowable property of the material cosmos as a whole, then we can hardly refuse to consider the theistic alternative. On this view, what sustains the world and each individual conscious

50. Johnston, *Saving God*, 131, emphasis added.

subject in existence is not the material cosmos, the vast concatenation of processes studied by physics, nor yet some hidden property of that material cosmos beyond the reach of physics, but the transcendent primordial and personal subject that is taken in traditional theism to be the source and sustainer of all being.

We cannot demonstrate or verify the truth of this picture—nor, for that matter, can we do so in the case of *any* metaphysical picture (including scientific materialism); for such pictures are not empirical hypotheses to be tested against evidence but fundamental frameworks of interpretation that form the backdrop for any possible hypotheses we may propose. But if the line of argument suggested in this chapter has been pointing in the right direction, the theistic framework is nevertheless one that is fundamentally hospitable to the reality of the "soul land" in which each of us finds him- or herself, in virtue of being an individual centre of conscious awareness and conceptual reflection. It is a framework that makes sense of those irreducible aspects of reality we cannot in integrity deny but which underpin the very meaning of our lives: the compelling values we encounter every day as we are confronted with beauty and goodness whose objective authority we are constrained to acknowledge whether we want to or not; and the vivid way in which the world is wondrously made present to us through the rich and precious gift of conscious experience.

The Partly Hidden Soul

To myself I am but darkness.

—NICOLAS MALEBRANCHE, *MÉDITATIONS CHRÉTIENNES ET MÉTAPHYSIQUES*

From Soul-Searching to Self-Fashioning

The notion of "soul" is freighted with multiple connotations that relate to different but interrelated aspects of the human condition—psychological, ethical, spiritual, and metaphysical. But as emphasized in the previous chapter, there is a common thread, insofar as when we use the term "soul" we are drawing attention to the fact that human beings are individual reflective subjects of conscious experience. Each of us is aware of him- or herself "from the inside," as it were, as "this *me* by which I am what I am." And in virtue of being self-aware subjects of this kind, we find ourselves at the centre of a "lifeworld" and have access to a whole rich domain of meaning and value. Finding the soul is thus not just a subjective exercise, an exercise in introspection and self-scrutiny; it is in part an outward-looking endeavour, an endeavour to understand our relation to the objective reality that confronts us and demands a response from us.

A long philosophical tradition regards the inward and the outward aspects of this search as closely intertwined. Augustine, at the close of the Roman Empire, followed in the Middle Ages by Bonaventure, and then again by Descartes in the early-modern period, was guided by the maxim *in interiore homine habitat veritas*—"the truth dwells within the inner human being." The thought here is that an interior descent, into the depths of the self, will lead us eventually towards the objective reality on which each individual self, and all existing things, ultimately depend.[1]

Our modern, largely secular, philosophical culture has little use for the theistic assumptions that underpin this Augustinian faith in descending within oneself as a route towards the truth. But perhaps paradoxically, the Enlightenment ideals of autonomy and authenticity seem to manifest even greater faith in the self, not simply as a staging post on the route to truth, as we find in Augustine and Descartes, but as the very source and determiner of truth and goodness. Thus, for Immanuel Kant, autonomy is "the basis of the dignity of human nature and of every rational nature," according to which our will must be considered as *selbstgesetzgebend* (giving the law to itself).[2] Building on this Kantian idea, the philosopher Christine Korsgaard, in our own time, has defined rational agency in terms of "self-constitution": "whenever you choose an action—whenever you take control of your own movements—you are constituting yourself as the author of that action, and so you are deciding who to be."[3] A more "aestheticized" version of the modern search for independence and authenticity, with its roots in Nietzsche rather than Kant, is proposed by Alexander Nehamas, when he argues that human life should be a project of "self-fashioning"—the search for that mode of living that expresses who we truly are, which

1. Augustine, *De vera religione*, ch. 39, 72. See also Bonaventure, *Itinerarium mentis in Deum* [1259], ch. 3, sec. 1; and Descartes, *Meditations*, Third Meditation, AT, vol. 7, 51; CSM, vol. 2, 35.

2. Kant, *Groundwork*, ch. 2, transl. Hill and Zweig, 236, 232.

3. Korsgaard, *Self-Constitution*, xi–xii.

may require each of us to "dislodge what was in place as the good and the true in order to find a place for himself, for his *own* truth and goodness."[4]

The contrast between the theistically inspired and the post-Enlightenment conceptions of the role of the self could not be more marked. For Augustine and Descartes, the "interior turn" was a route to the truth, and ultimately a way of reaching the soul's true destiny, only insofar as the individual soul was taken to be made in the image of the creator, the source of all truth. "Go back into your inner self, where dwells the truth," says Augustine; "let us return to ourselves, into our mind," says Bonaventure, that we may search for the "light of truth shining in our minds"; "I turn my mind's eye upon myself," says Descartes, and find the idea of God stamped there, like the "mark the craftsman has set on his work."[5] In all three thinkers, what is recommended is a turn away from the misleading and deceptive world of outward sensory perception in order to direct the gaze on the innate truths implanted in the soul by God. And crucially, all three regard the mind or soul as responsive to a truth and goodness that it did not create, but of which, provided the attention is directed aright, it has clear and transparent awareness. In the modern vision, by contrast, the soul cannot rely on divine assistance from outside, but must instead "constitute itself" by choosing actions that represent its most authentic self-expression. We can see a kind of compressed version of this shift in the trajectory of a single lifetime, that of Kant, who moved from faith in the "objective reality" of God as a "postulate of

4. Nehamas, *Art of Living*, 183.

5. Augustine, *De vera religione*, ch. 39, 72; Bonaventure, *Itinerarium mentis in Deum* [1259], ch. 3, sec. 1; and Descartes, *Meditations*, Third Meditation, AT, vol. 7, 51; CSM, vol. 2, 35.

practical reason"[6] to the view affirmed in his last work, unfinished at his death, that God is "not a substance outside myself," but rather "I, man, am this being myself."[7]

In the characteristically modern vision embraced by Kant at the close of his life, the self is essentially on its own: there is nothing God can do for us "from the outside," as it were. As Christopher Insole has put it, "our main hope must be in ourselves and in our reason."[8] It is an open question whether the resulting vision of independence and autonomy represents a truer conception of the human condition than the vision of dependency that underlies the traditional theistic picture of the mind as relying on "external" divine illumination. But whatever their respective attractions, neither vision can claim to be self-evidently or demonstrably superior; indeed both turn out under scrutiny to be vulnerable to a certain kind of epistemic circularity.

For a theist such as Descartes, there can be no independent guarantee that the "clear and distinct ideas" supposedly implanted in the soul by God reflect the truth; to argue that they must be true because they are divinely implanted requires one first to prove the existence of God, which can only be done using those same allegedly implanted truths—this is the notorious problem of the "Cartesian circle."[9] But equally, the more modern Kantian vision of independent human rationality and autonomy lacks any principled reason why the determinations of the "rational will" can be trusted to guide us towards what is true and good. For there are, notoriously, many conflicting blueprints that

6. Kant, *Critique of Practical Reason*, pt. 1, bk. 2, ch. 2, sec. 5.

7. Kant, *Opus postumum*, Transl. Förster and Rosen, 230. See also Insole, *Intolerable God*, 132.

8. Insole, *Intolerable God*, 147.

9. See Cottingham, *Descartes*, 66–70.

humans have devised for living their lives, or for constructing the ideal society, all allegedly representing what is the "rational" choice. Kantian ethics does, to be sure, endeavour to place a constraint on rational choice—namely, that "principles are to be found for a plurality of . . . agents who share a world . . . [and] who cannot base this sharing on adopting unsharable principles."[10] But for all the attractions of this liberal framework, the Kantian constraint (you may only rationally will what can be accepted by all) is one that cannot claim universal rational appeal, since there are, notoriously, those bent on power who simply refuse to prioritize the ideals of free cooperative debate and shareable principles in this way.

Given the darker side of our human nature, the inescapable desire to control and dominate, Kant's assertion at the end of his life that "I, man, am this divine being myself" could be interpreted in a sinister light, as paving the way for a hubristic post-Hegelian world picture, where human beings see themselves as the supreme manifestation of the *Weltgeist* or "world spirit," taking control of history, and in a certain way arrogating to themselves divine or quasi-divine status.[11] This is the seductive but dangerous idea that is prefigured in the temptation of the serpent narrated in the Genesis story—"ye shall be as Gods."[12] So Kant's notion of "self-legislation," of humanity left essentially on its own, is fraught with problems. For unless human reason is an "instrument of transcendence"[13]—that is, able to

10. The formulation is from O'Neil, *Constructions of Reason*, 27.

11. See Hegel, *Phenomenology of Spirit.*

12. Genesis 3:5. It should be noted that in some strands of Eastern Orthodox theological thought the words of the serpent, "ye shall be as gods," are interpreted not so much as a temptation leading to the Fall as pointing to *theosis* or divinization as the ultimate destiny towards which humankind is called to progress.

13. This term was first introduced by Thomas Nagel, in *Mind and Cosmos*, 85.

discern an objective, independent moral order—then it is far from clear how the decrees generated by the rational will can have the requisite normative authority. This is the difficulty underlying the more recent efforts to defend self-legislation referred to above, such as putting the weight on "self-constitution"—"finding a role and fulfilling it with dedication"[14]—or "authenticity," being true to one's deepest self. To borrow two Cartesian metaphors, the soul left to its own devices is often prone to tumble around in a "bottomless whirlpool," or in "inextricable darkness."[15]

But there is a more fundamental problem that seems to beset both the traditional theistic and the modern, secular Enlightenment quests for truth and goodness, whether by self-searching or by self-fashioning. And that is that both seem to presuppose that the reflective human mind can make rational choices based on a transparent and unproblematic access to its own contents. The shakiness of this presupposition has been acutely explored in the many literary depictions of protagonists who turn out to have been fundamentally mistaken about their own deepest desires and truest reasons (Elizabeth Bennett in *Pride and Prejudice* and Helen Graham in *The Tenant of Wildfell Hall* are among the striking examples from nineteenth-century literature).[16] This is not to say that the search for one's true self is doomed to failure; but it needs to be recognized that the task may be immensely more problematic than many philosophical conceptions of a life mapped out by rationally enlightened choice might suggest. A great deal of philosophical ethics is spent talking about "practical reason," "reasons for action," and the rationally

14. Korsgaard, *Self-Constitution*, 25.

15. Descartes, *Meditations*, First Meditation, AT, vol. 7, 23; CSM, vol. 2, 15; and Second Meditation, AT, vol. 7, 24; CSM, vol. 2, 16.

16. The first by Jane Austen (1813); the second by Anne Bronte (1848).

ordered "projects" that constitute the good life. And the assumption often made here is that the mind is like a transparent goldfish bowl: the agent consults a schedule of his or her goals and desires and calculates the best means to implement them. Yet what if the soul is largely opaque: what if much of it is a dark area even to the subject who looks within? What if the mind's own judgement is often clouded by distortions and projections of which it is only dimly aware? We have had occasion many times to refer to Descartes's suggestive phrase "this *me* [*ce moi*] by which I am what I am." But what if this "me," this lordly Ego, is an impostor, a pretender to an exalted rational status to which it has no straightforward title?[17] What if, to quote the famous challenge posed by Sigmund Freud in the early part of the twentieth century, "the 'I' is not even master in his own house, but must remain content with the veriest scraps of information about what is going on unconsciously in his own mind?"[18] To the implications of this psychoanalytic challenge, and how it bears on the project of "finding the soul," we must now turn.

The Opacity of the Soul and Psychic Integration

Psychoanalytic theory, in the years since its foundations were established by Freud, has received more than its fair share of criticism from philosophers, particularly those of an analytic persuasion. The charges levelled have included logical ones (about the alleged incoherence of some of the concepts employed) and methodological ones (about alleged failure to meet scientific

17. Cf. Lacan, *Four Fundamental Concepts*, 263.

18. Freud, *Introductory Lectures on Psychoanalysis*, ch. 18, 326. For a highly stimulating discussion of the "return of the soul" in various psychoanalytic thinkers, see Tyler, *Pursuit of the Soul*, chs. 5 and 6.

standards of repeatability and verifiability).[19] But whatever one makes of these debates, at the heart of the psychoanalytic view of the human condition lie two very simple, and very persuasive, notions.

The first is the pivotal insight of Freud that the contents of the mind—the all-too-familiar desires and beliefs that appear so transparently accessible to introspection—are in many cases subject to a pervasive ambiguity and opacity. Often they turn out to carry hidden charges of significance, glimpsed, if at all, only dimly and imperfectly, at the very edge of conscious awareness: here is the key to Freud's claim that the Ego can no longer be supposed to be master in its own house. It is a notion that is obviously a disturbing one, but is also, as Freud brilliantly demonstrated through his case histories, an endlessly fertile one for the continuing project of trying to understand ourselves better and to live more healthy lives.

The second idea, particularly associated with the insights of Carl Jung, is actually closely related: that psychological growth and maturity requires us, at some point in our lives, to delve down into the dark recesses of the mind, confront the shadowy side of our nature, and then to set about the long and painful process of coming to terms with it—the process Jung called "individuation." As he explained:

> The psychoanalytic aim is to observe the shadowy presentations—whether in the form of images or of feelings—that are spontaneously evolved in the psyche and appear, without his or her bidding, to the person who looks within. In this way we find once more what we have repressed or forgotten. Painful though it may be, this is itself a

---

19. See further Cottingham, *Philosophy and the Good Life*, ch. 4, sec. 2.

gain—for what is inferior or even worthless belongs to me as my shadow, and gives me substance and mass. How can I be substantial if I fail to cast a shadow? I must have a dark side if I am to be whole; and inasmuch as I become conscious of my own shadow, I also remember that I am a human being like any other.[20]

There are powerful resonances here that poets and playwrights had explored many centuries before Freud and Jung—for the genius of these two great thinkers was that they managed to bring to light and make explicit truths that in a sense we had known all along. There is a beautiful image of individuation or integration in Shakespeare's *The Tempest*, where Prospero, the archetypal self, finds the grace to "break his staff," the symbol of power,[21] and to abjure the Ego's futile efforts to dominate and control. This finally allows him to come to terms with the character who is in a way a projection or externalization of part of himself, the wretched savage Caliban—the repulsive and unruly counterpart of Prospero's other companion, the celestial spirit Ariel. Having berated and cursed Caliban throughout the play, ordering him about and trying to curb and suppress him, Prospero (in one of the play's most moving moments, if it is done well) reaches out to him and humbly confesses to the silent crowd of onlookers: "This thing of darkness I acknowledge mine."[22]

The struggle for wholeness, the process of what Jung calls individuation, has an obvious relevance to the theme broached at

20. Jung, "Problems of Modern Psychotherapy," 40; translation slightly adapted to make the phrasing more gender neutral.

21. Shakespeare, *The Tempest* [1610], act 5, scene 1; the image comes in the famous speech where Prospero swears to resign his magical powers.

22. Shakespeare, *The Tempest*, act 5, scene 1.

the start of chapter 1 and frequently resurfacing in subsequent chapters: the task of finding one's true self—the self one is meant to be. Expressed in religious terms, this is the struggle for moral and spiritual integrity, and it is clear from a host of scriptural texts that the Judaeo-Christian tradition places great importance on a unified or integrated life. In one of the Psalms, we find the prayer "Give me, O Lord, an undivided heart," a petition for a psychological and ethical unity.[23] The Gospels speak of the importance of finding one's *true self*. Even gaining the whole world is not enough to compensate for the loss of oneself (*heautos*), says a famous passage in St Luke.[24] A few chapters later in the same Gospel, we find the story of the prodigal son, who goes off to a distant land and squanders his inheritance, but one day wakes up and "comes to himself" (*eis heauton elthōn*).[25] As the Dominican writer Timothy Radcliffe persuasively interprets it, the prodigal's decision to go back to his home and family is really the same as rediscovering his true self, "since his exile from his family is an exile from his true identity as son and brother. He can only find himself again with them."[26] For any human being, the failure to find oneself, and indeed the risk of imperceptibly losing oneself, one's very soul, is the gravest possible danger, the "sickness unto death" described by Kierkegaard.[27]

The value of the psychoanalytic perspective is that it confronts unflinchingly the true complexity and difficulty of the task

23. Psalm 86:11. In Hebrew the psalmist prays to God, "*yahed levavi*"—literally, "unite my heart!" (the imperative verb *yahed* comes from the root *ehad*, meaning one).

24. Luke 9:25.

25. Luke 15:17.

26. Radcliffe, *Why Go to Church*, 20. See also Cottingham, "Integrity and Fragmentation."

27. See above, ch. 1, "The Risk of Loss."

described in the Gospels and in Kierkegaard—the task of finding and being true to oneself. If the mind were a transparent
goldfish bowl whose contents were all readily accessible to conscious introspection, then it might perhaps be thought a relatively straightforward matter to identify the most important
beliefs and desires that constitute my core self, and to make sure
they are centre stage in my deliberations and choices. But if the
true nature and character of many of my beliefs and desires are
shrouded in ambiguity and obscurity and often concealed from
direct awareness even from me, the deliberating subject, then the
task of managing my life in the way that is faithful to my best and
truest self emerges as a truly formidable undertaking. From a
religious perspective, indeed, the difficulty seems to be a twofold
one. In the first place, in religious terms, the task of finding one's
true self entails recovering the sense of "existing before God," in
Kierkegaard's phrase.[28] But the God before whom we are required to present ourselves is very far from being plainly in view
(a point we shall return to in the last section of this chapter).
Jewish and Christian believers have long wrestled with the problem that their God is a "hidden God"—a phrase that goes right
back to Isaiah.[29] But on top of this first difficulty we now have a
second one: the human soul, traditionally taken to bear the
image of God, so that individual mind or spirit is a faint and finite reflection of the divine—that very soul itself turns out to be
hidden, its nature and contents partly occluded from conscious
awareness. In short, from a theistic perspective the quest is for a
hidden God; and it has to be undertaken by a partly hidden self.

And yet neither in the Gospels nor in the long catalogue of
subsequent spiritual writings has it ever been suggested that the
existential and moral task of finding the true self is an easy one.

28. Kierkegaard, *Sickness unto Death*, 79.
29. Isaiah 45:15.

On the contrary, from St Paul through Augustine and down to Kierkegaard and beyond, the search for authentic selfhood before God has been seen as a lifelong existential and moral struggle.[30] Even Immanuel Kant, the apostle of rational enlightenment, speaks darkly of "the hell of self-cognition" and remarks that only a descent into these hellish depths can "pave the way to godliness."[31] This struggle is clearly going to be all the more complicated given that it involves materials that are often not plainly in view, but need to be dragged painfully into the light in the teeth of all sorts of evasion and resistance; but in the end none of this is radically inconsistent with a traditional theistic account of the human condition, and hence the basic psychoanalytic idea of the opacity of the human psyche is one that theists can readily accept. It is an idea that is worth taking on board in any case, whether or not we are theists, since it plays a crucial role in the project of "finding the soul" and in the journey towards moral and psychological integrity. Giving up the notion of the mind as transparent and fully accessible to the scrutiny of reason may be the first step towards the healing of the human psyche. Put in secular terms, this will be an indispensable part of the quest for a fulfilled and meaningful life. And in theistic terms, as we shall see, it may allow space for a better sense of how the human psyche is able to reach towards the divine.

The Depths of the Psyche

Despite the disputes and controversies surrounding psychoanalytic theory, the basic idea of the opacity of the human psyche draws support from a number of directions, including the philosophical and the scientific. On the philosophical side, René

30. Romans 7:21; Augustine, *Confessions*, passim, esp. bk. 8.
31. Kant, *Metaphysic of Morals*, 191.

Descartes, who is often supposed to be the champion of the idea of the perfect transparency of the mind to itself, did in fact maintain that a good deal of our mental life, particularly that concerned with the emotions and the passions, is subject to significant indistinctness and obscurity. In a striking anticipation of Freud, Descartes pointed out that the nature and operation of passions such as love is often hard for us to understand, because our adult awareness is often infected by "confused feelings" going back to our childhood, which can cloud and distort our subsequent rational judgement, without our being fully conscious of what is going on.[32] More radically still, as flagged in the opening epigraph for the present chapter, we find Descartes's religiously devout disciple Nicolas Malebranche taking issue with the master by insisting that not just some of the contents but even the nature or essence of the soul are obscure to us: "To myself I am but darkness [*Je ne suis que ténèbres à moi meme*], and my own substance seems something which is beyond my understanding."[33]

Jumping forward to modern scientific studies of the workings of the mind, there has been increasing interest in recent years in the "archaeology of belief," as the British theologian Graham Ward has called it—in what lies beneath the surface when we believe something. It is becoming increasingly clear that believing or disbelieving something involves far more complex and multilayered processes than may be apparent to the subject as she rationally evaluates the relevant evidence. There are much "deeper layers of embodied engagement and reaction"

32. Descartes, letter to Chanut, 1 February 1647, AT, vol. 4, 606; CSMK, 308. See also Cottingham, *Cartesian Reflections*, ch. 1, sec. 4(b).

33. Malebranche, *Méditations chrétiennes et métaphysiques*, ch. 9, sec. 15. See further Cottingham, *Rationalists*, 154–55; 220, n. 67.

involved, where we are touched "imaginatively, affectively and existentially."[34] Drawing on empirical research into the behavioural and neurological underpinnings of belief and its evolutionary and prehistoric roots, Ward delves into the domain of what the Berkeley psychologist John Kihlstrom has termed the "cognitive unconscious."[35] A rich array of non-conscious mental activity—including learned responses that have become automatic, subliminal perceptions that influence our conscious judgements, and implicit but not consciously recalled memories—profoundly affects how we perceive and interpret the world.[36]

There is thus a fair amount of consensus from different quarters as to the surprisingly limited extent of our direct conscious access into the nature and workings of the human mind; and all of this is of course strikingly consistent with the basic Freudian insight that our conscious deliberations and reflections are only the thinnest of surfaces overlaying a powerful array of unconscious mental activity. Yet, so far from clashing with the view of the self espoused in a traditional theistic outlook, these results seem to find a ready home there. So, for example, in the quest to find one's true self and to learn to live with sincerity and integrity, it will be no surprise that the struggles and difficulties of the analysand under the probing of the therapist in the consulting room turn out to be not wholly dissimilar from the struggles of the novice under the guidance of a spiritual director. The search for moral growth and integrity (which on the Jungian model is the fundamental goal of psychoanalysis) can be seen

34. Ward, *Unbelievable*, 7, 10, 31.

35. Kihlstrom, "Cognitive Unconscious"; see also Kahneman, *Thinking Fast and Slow*, ch. 1.

36. Ward, *Unbelievable*, 11, 68.

in religious terms as the hard and painful struggle to bring the interior recesses of the soul before God, so that what is amiss can be purified or reshaped in the process of spiritual rebirth and transformation. As was argued many decades ago by Victor White, one of the first writers to see strong parallels between the psychoanalytic and the spiritual journey: "psychological analysis is seldom successful unless it brings about something . . . not unlike . . . contrition . . . a radical change of the patient's conscious outlook, a *metanoia* or change of mind, and with it of his moral valuations and behaviour."[37]

White was strongly influenced by Jungian ideas, and Jung himself was of course sympathetic to religion, in contrast to Freud, who famously dismissed the religious impulse as an infantile longing for protection and security.[38] This difference in attitudes is reflected in a corresponding difference in Freud's and Jung's approaches to the therapeutic process. For Jung, healing is achieved in part by a letting be, a surrender of the Ego, so that our imagination is allowed to be spontaneously energized by the archetypal forms innate in the human psyche; and Jung maintains that religious imagery and symbolism perform a vital function here.[39] Part of the reason for this is that the process of individuation requires modes of thought and expression that operate not just on the surface level of explicit assertion, but also carry deep imaginative resonances for our psychological balance and harmony. To give but one example, the figure of Christ functions for Jung as an "archetype of the self," a powerfully resonant image of the perfectly unified and integrated human being.[40] From this

---

37. White, *God and the Unconscious*, 187.
38. Freud, *Civilization and Its Discontents*, 260.
39. See Jung, *Symbols of Transformation*.
40. See Jung, *Aion*, 183. See also Jung, *Psychology and Religion*, 89–95.

perspective, as Michael Palmer aptly puts it in his account of the Jungian position:

> Religion, far from being neurotic, is revealed as a constant and evolving process in the development of the psychic personality. . . . Religious symbols . . . open up a psychic level . . . that is primordial and . . . of supreme value for the present and future development of the human psyche.[41]

For Freud, by contrast, the basic mechanism of the therapeutic process, and the goal towards which it is directed, involves the sorry remnants of our psychological past being dragged painfully into the daylight and laid out for inspection, to be diagnosed and analysed by the clear light of reason. As Freud's famous motto has it: "*Wo Es war, soll Ich werden*" (where Id was, there shall Ego be).[42] Freud's conception of the healing process is an essentially rationalistic one;[43] or as Jonathan Lear diagnoses it, rather more astringently, in a recent study: "Freud was himself in the grip of a wishful Enlightenment fantasy—an illusion of the future—in which the inexorable march of reason, 'our God *Logos*,' overcomes religious superstition with the fatal inevitability of a process of growth."[44]

To take issue with Freud's hyper-rationalism is not of course to disparage his seminal insights into the nature of the human mind; it is simply to say that there is nothing in those insights that requires anyone to go along with his very logocentric view of what constitutes a healthy psyche, or to embrace the reductive and dismissive attitude to religious thinking that goes along

41. Palmer, *Freud and Jung*, 110–11.
42. Freud, *New Lectures on Psychoanalysis*, lecture 31.
43. Cottingham, *Philosophy and the Good Life*, ch. 4, sec. 8.
44. Lear, *Wisdom Won from Illness*, 203.

with it. The following section will look further at the connection between the psychoanalytic search to find one's true, integrated self, and the religious search to find, or at least reach towards, the mysterious source and ground of goodness and truth in relation to which, on the traditional theistic picture, the soul can hope to find fulfilment and completion.

Before proceeding, it may be worth adding a (perhaps overdue) word about the status of the theistic language making its appearance here and in many other places in our argument. As was indicated at the close of the previous chapter, the use of such language should not be taken as a claim that the truth of the theistic framework can be verified or demonstrated. The point rather is that we should be open to the possibility that a theistic framework might be a helpful way of interpreting certain fundamental aspects of our humanity, in particular those relating to what has been called the "soul." Thus, the suggestion that emerged from the previous chapter was that a theistic framework is hospitable to accommodating our status as "souls"—subjective centres of conscious reflective awareness—and our resulting ability to inhabit the soul's "lifeworld" and thereby gain access to a rich domain of irreducible meaning and value. Neither this suggestion, nor any of the other considerations offered in this book, should be construed as offering "arguments for the existence of God" in the traditional sense in which that notion is understood in the philosophy of religion.

There are, to be sure, fair numbers of philosophers working today who think there is nothing wrong with these traditional arguments, or who think they can be suitably revised or adapted to offer demonstrative or at least probabilistic proofs of God's existence. On the other side, there are those (probably much larger) numbers who follow the "Enlightenment" line that it is pointless, or philosophically off limits, to make knowledge claims about the nature of the "ultimate reality" underlying the phenomenal world. But the debate between the supporters and the opponents of the Enlightenment position is not one that needs to be adjudicated for the purposes of our present discussion. What does need to be said is that the Enlightenment strictures about venturing beyond the phenomenal world (Kant), or about speculating on the "ultimate springs and principles of nature" (Hume), are about the limits of discursive *knowledge*, not about the possible limits of *reality*. Hume, a professed sceptic, could not and would not pronounce about the existence or non-existence of such "ultimate springs and principles," but simply asserted that they were "forever shut up from human curiosity and inquiry."[45] And Kant, in demolishing the pretentions of reason to soar above the phenomenal world, was nevertheless clear that we have an idea of God, and that God is a proper object of faith.[46]

Whatever the limits of human knowledge may be, it cannot be denied that the *idea* of God at least retains a hold on us, believers or not. If human beings ceased to reach beyond themselves, to hope for something more than to solve the mundane problems of their quotidian existence, then the questing spirit that is the very soul of every human being, the signature of our humanity, would have died. If humans ceased to have the idea of God, at least as a question, then, as the theologian Karl Rahner puts it:

Man would never face the totality of the world and of himself helplessly, silently and anxiously . . . he would remain mired *in* the world and *in* himself, and no longer go through that mysterious process which he *is*. Man would have forgotten the totality and its ground, and at the same time, if we can put it this

45. Hume, *Enquiry concerning Human Understanding*, sec. 4, pt. 1.

46. Kant, *Critique of Pure Reason*, B, xxx. See further Firestone and Jacobs, *Defense of Kant's Religion*.

way, would have forgotten that he had forgotten. What would it be like? We can only say: he would have ceased being a man. He would have regressed to the level of a clever animal. . . . Man really exists as man only when he uses the word "God" at least as a question. . . . The absolute death of the word "God," including even the eradication of its past, would be the signal, no longer heard by anyone, that man himself had died.[47]

The Soul's Hidden Yearning for God

The idea of God is linked to the human longing for meaning, the yearning for completion. Is this anxious longing, as Rahner suggests in the passage just quoted, inseparable from our very humanity? For Freud the desire indicates a pathology, rather like a case of arrested development, a neurotic or at least infantile manifestation of a helpless and irrational longing for magical protection in the face of the inevitable perils and insecurities of human life. And the right response to such a pathology, for Freud, is to identify its aetiology, using the scientific tools of psychoanalysis, with the goal of helping the analysand to emerge into rational adulthood—a condition of enlightenment where we give up the fantasy of divine protection and face up to the unavoidable facts of human existence. This will not of course guarantee happiness, or foreclose the possibility that life may go badly, but at least it will free us from the degrading grip of an infantile illusion. Freud's aim, as one of his best known remarks explains, is to eliminate *neurotic* misery, without claiming to deal with the residue of *ordinary* misery.[48]

47. Rahner, *Foundations of Christian Faith*, 46–50.

48. "Much will be gained if we succeed in transforming your hysterical misery into common unhappiness. With a mental life that has been restored to health, you will be better armed against that unhappiness." Freud, *Studies in Hysteria*, 305.

The contrast with Jung, when it comes to the allegedly infantile or neurotic nature of the desire for God, could not be
greater. For Jung construes the human desire for God as deriv-
ing from an innate archetype, lodged deep within the collective
unconscious of the human psyche, an ultimately benign presence that offers the key to our healing and wholeness. The
presence of such an archetype is not, incidentally, supposed to
provide proof of or evidence for the existence of God—Jung
remains resolutely neutral here, refusing to pronounce upon
the metaphysical question of the objective reality of God:

> We know that God-images play a great role in psychology, but
> we cannot prove the [actual] existence of God.... To me, per-
> sonally speaking, the question whether God exists at all or
> not is futile. I am sufficiently convinced of the effects man has
> always attributed to a divine being. I am well satisfied with the
> fact that I know experiences which I cannot avoid calling nu-
> minous or divine.[49]

But despite Jung's metaphysical caution, what we can reasonably
take from his writings on religion is the idea that an inchoate
longing for God, buried deep within the human psyche, is a primordial part of our nature, and that when the associated ener-
gizing images of the divine are allowed to surface they are able
to play a vital role in the flourishing of the human soul and its
growth towards maturity and wholeness.

To construe the desire for God as rooted in primordial arche-
types implanted deep in the mind below the level of explicit
rational awareness may at first seem inimical to the expectation
or requirement found in many theistic frameworks (including
Catholic and Anglican Christianity) that belief in God should

---

49. From correspondence with H. L. Philp, 1956, repr. in Jung, *Collected Works*,
vol. 18, 706–7; quoted in Palmer, *Freud and Jung*, 125.

be not *merely* a matter of instinct or faith (important though these are), but should also be in some way rationally grounded. But a lot hinges here on what one means by "rationally grounded." The methodology of contemporary analytic philosophy tends to regard a given position as soundly based just insofar as its content, and all the supporting elements, enjoy maximal precisification, with everything laid out clearly in view and all ambiguity eliminated. As Raymond Geuss has pointed out, ambiguity is "regarded as a grave defect in propositional forms of investigation and argumentation," and many disciplines "emphasise the need to adopt the most stringent measure to eliminate [it] as completely as possible."[50] Yet reflection suggests that something can be rationally grounded in the sense of being a reasonable belief, supported by experience and harmonizing with other parts of our experience, without the supporting grounds being transparently analysable in propositional terms.

For example, it is reasonable for me to believe that I really "get on" with someone, that I have a direct bond or rapport with that person, even though I cannot specify a list of properties or qualities in virtue of which this is the case; indeed, there is no need even for me to have direct conscious awareness of what it is that makes us "click," as the phrase goes. Someone might try to specify a list of common interests or shared tastes in order to explain or describe this kind of rapport, yet though it may well be possible to draw up such a list, the listable items are clearly neither necessary nor sufficient for the rapport to exist: Andrew may belong to the same clubs or associations as Belinda and share the same outlook on a whole range of topics, yet somehow the two do not "click"; and, conversely, the relationship may "take off" despite a wide divergence in interests and pursuits. To avoid any

50. Geuss, "Poetry and Knowledge," 8. Cf. Empson, *Seven Types of Ambiguity*.

misunderstanding here, there is no need to suppose that the "rapport" in this example has to be one of sexual attraction; one may simply be thinking of the ingredients of a warm and friendly human relationship. When two people just "get on," as we say, when they enjoy each other's company and look forward to their meetings as not just furthering their projects or careers or interests, but as having a special sort of personal and emotional significance, it is reasonable to think that there are all sorts of affectively charged cues and interactions, voice tones, eye contact, empathetic responses, facial expressions, bodily gestures, and much more, that facilitate and foster their pleasure in each other's company; yet all or most of these may operate well below the threshold of conscious awareness. This is not to deny that there are many factors that could be consciously catalogued and specified by the parties involved; but it seems likely that these transparently accessible features of the relationship are not ultimately what gives it life and energy as a friendship. It is "what lies beneath" that really makes the difference, and that turns an enjoyable encounter between like-minded associates into a genuine rapport, the stuff of which authentic friendships are made.[51]

For the believer, our experience of the divine will be seen as in some ways analogous to this. The "grandeur of God" that "will flame out like shining from shook foil," as Gerard Manley Hopkins vividly expresses it,[52] is something responded to at an immediate and intuitive level, below the threshold of what can be consciously mapped out and catalogued. It is an affectively toned, emotionally energized, joyful response to the natural world that is activated deep down in layers of the mind that are only hinted and guessed at by the conscious rational intellect.

51. See further Cottingham, "Engagement, Immersion and Enactment."
52. Hopkins, "God's Grandeur" [1877], in *Poems and Prose*, 27.

Moreover, when Hopkins classes such experiences as experiences of the divine, he does not at all have to be understood as claiming that what is presented is empirical evidence that warrants the inference of the existence of a divine creator behind the natural world. There is no such "evidence"; or at least none that meets the "neutral-spectator" standards of science.[53] Rather, what is involved is a holistic response, a response of the whole person; something, to be sure, that entails conscious awareness on the subject's part as it is happening (otherwise Hopkins could never have gone on to write his poem), but something that, like so much human belief and desire, takes shape prior to, not subsequent to, anything classifiable by the reflective conscious mind. Just as Andrew and Belinda directly experience their relationship as a friendship, so too the poet, and the many thousands of readers who have felt the same, directly experience the world as infused and transfigured with the divine.

Now of course there is an obvious disanalogy here between the type of case described by Hopkins and our example of an ordinary human relationship—namely, that when one is friends with someone, he or she is clearly in view, able to be seen and heard, to be embraced or shaken by the hand; whereas God, as Paul's letter to Timothy has it, dwells in "light inaccessible, whom no human being has seen or can see."[54] Nevertheless, there remains a significant point of contact between the human and the divine cases. When I love someone, truly love them for themselves as opposed to desiring to possess them, there is necessarily something I cannot, and should not try to, encompass. They remain "other," as Emmanuel Levinas and others have

53. See Moser, *Elusive God*, 47. See also Moser, *Evidence for God*.
54. 1 Timothy 6:16.

put it[55]—in a certain way holy or sacred, and beyond my reach; and indeed the respecting of that sacred space, even in the most intimate relationships, is in the end the key to the relationship's flourishing. The holiness of the divine seems like this, though infinitely more so: it cannot be approach or encompassed, because it remains ultimately incomprehensible.

So how can God be an object of love, as it is supposed to be in the Judaeo-Christian tradition? Precisely, I would suggest, in virtue of the inchoate human longing for the infinite good that is unencompassable, forever out of reach, yet forever beckoning us forward to transcend ourselves. Unlike conscious desires for ordinary goods, which have a clearly specified object, and which have satisfaction conditions, the desire for God is an open-ended yearning buried deep below the levels of propositionally shaped cognition that mark out the rational conscious mind.

The experiences described by poets and spiritual writers as pointing towards the divine—for example, experiences of the beauties of the natural world, or of the self-giving and transformative love between two people—have the form not of data gathered to support a certain conclusion, but of intimations, "hints and guesses," in T. S. Eliot's phrase.[56] Their mysterious character, welling up from something deep within us that eludes conscious grasp, carries the hallmark of the sacred precisely insofar as it directs us to something that remains out of reach.

In a separate poem (probably lesser known than his "God's Grandeur," mentioned above), Hopkins speaks of our responses to physical beauty—beauty of form in another human being—and he reflects on its arousing or "dangerous" aspects, as he calls

55. Levinas, *Totality and Infinity*.

56. T. S. Eliot, "The Dry Salvages" [1941], line 212; subsequently incorporated into *Four Quartets* [1943].

them: "To what serves mortal beauty—dangerous; does set dancing blood . . .". The poem is one in which it is all too easy for the condescending reader to detect the marks of repressed sexuality. But whatever may or may not have been the celibate poet's personal torments, the crux of the poem lies in its subsequent reflections on the Christian ideal of love:

> To man, that needs would worship block or barren stone
> Our law says: Love what are love's worthiest, were all
>   known
> World's loveliest—men's selves. Self flashes off frame
>   and face.[57]

The love that is commanded in the Christian ideal is not the love that is a desire to possess, but a loving recognition of the unencompassable *self* that shines forth from someone's physical presence—the self that "flashes off frame and face." And behind such truest and best human love lies the love of God, the ungraspable primordial self, which similarly "flashes off" from the beauties of the natural world, or as the earlier "God's Grandeur" poem has it, "flames out like shining from shook foil."

We do not fully understand what is going on in our minds and hearts when we respond to these intimations of the divine. But there seems to me a good case for saying that in the forward, open-ended, exalted movement of the soul, in the primal yearning rooted deep in the unconscious mind, we get to the heart of what spiritual experience is all about. What is going on may not be fully describable by reason, or fully accessible to consciousness, but as an undeniable feature of our human experience it nevertheless forms part of the perfectly reasonable grounds for faith, as well as being fully consistent with what we are daily

57. Hopkins, "To What Serves Mortal Beauty?" in *Poems and Prose*, 58.

learning through science about the complexities and opacity of the human belief system. None of this, of course, amounts to a coercive argument for theistic belief; but it perhaps gets us fractionally closer to seeing how a dependent human being, by delving deep into the recesses of the partly hidden soul, may reach forward towards the partly hidden God.

The Soul and the Transcendent

Who hath desired the Sea—the immense and contemptuous
   surges?
The shudder, the stumble, the swerve ere the star-stabbing
   bowsprit emerges—
The orderly clouds of the Trades and the ridged roaring
   sapphire thereunder—
Unheralded cliff-lurking flaws and the head-sails' low-
   volleying thunder?
His Sea in no wonder the same—his Sea and the same in
   each wonder . . .
His Sea that his being fulfils?
So and no otherwise—so and no otherwise hill-men desire
   their hills!

—RUDYARD KIPLING, *KIM*

Reaching Forward to the Transcendent

Kipling's lines hint at that powerful longing of the human soul on
which we reflected at the end of the previous chapter, a longing
whose open-ended and in some ways indistinct nature sorts
well with the complexity and depth of the human psyche, so
much of which is hidden from direct view. The lines somehow
manage to conjure up something of the yearning of the finite
creature for what is infinitely beyond its grasp; and as so often

in poetry, resonances operating beneath the level of our explicit conscious awareness convey much more than could be stated in a set of literal propositions. The point of the poem is not just that seafaring folk have a strong desire to go to sea, or that those born in the hills welcome the chance to return there. The ocean in a certain way stands for that which is vastly greater than us, overwhelmingly fearful and majestic, awful in its power, a nexus of ever-changing wonder that is nevertheless "the same in each wonder." And beyond that, what the seafarer longs for is not just an expanse of salt water, but "his sea that his being fulfils"—that which will bring meaning and completion to his existence. And "so and no otherwise," as the closing line of the verse affirms, do the "hill-men desire their hills."[1] In Kipling's novel *Kim*, in which this verse forms the epigraph to one of the closing chapters, the hills rising mysteriously above the plain represent, for the aged lama to whom Kim has attached himself as disciple, the ultimate source and goal of his lifelong spiritual quest.

The poetic imagery Kipling employs may not resonate with every reader; but among those fortunate enough to have leisure to reflect on these matters, there will be few if any who would not acknowledge that something like the strange longing in question has made itself felt at some stage in their lives, perhaps in a moving encounter with a great work of art or architecture, perhaps through the extraordinary power of music, perhaps in deep emotions of wonder and harmony evoked by the natural world around us, or perhaps the unfathomable mystery of closeness with one we love. The fact that such experiences are so hard to describe in the dry factual language of literal truth only reinforces the need for philosophy, if it is to have any

---

1. Kipling, *Kim*, ch. 12.

pretentions to come to terms with the mystery and complexity of the human condition, to draw on additional resources than those available via the austere tools of logical analysis, invaluable and indispensable though those tools are.

These richer resources are afforded by the creative and imaginative arts, and by the human mind itself when it allows itself space for the kind of open listening and attunement that is crowded out in our daily dealings with the necessities of life. In such moments, what wells up within us is an inchoate desire buried deep within the human soul—the longing of the weak and imperfect and confused human spirit for something it cannot fully grasp, but of which it has vivid intimations in those elusive but powerfully moving human experiences often called "spiritual."

Insofar as these reflections can be seen as pointing in a theistic direction, they harmonize with some of our results in chapter 3, which ended by suggesting that a theistic framework, with its picture of an infinite primordial consciousness at the heart of reality, offers some kind of interpretative handle on the otherwise deeply perplexing relation between subjective consciousness and objective reality. It was also suggested in the same chapter that a theistic outlook is hospitable to two striking features of the reality we encounter in our ordinary human lives: the irreducible nature of conscious experience—the "life-world" accessible to each individual subject—and the irreducible normative requirements to which, like it or not, we are subject as moral beings and which continually demand a response from us.

Any account of the human condition must sooner or later come to terms with these irreducible aspects of our experience, those aspects in connection with which people have often made use of the notion of "soul." But what is really meant by the term "irreducible," which is so often employed in this sort of context, and which has made frequent appearances in our own earlier discussions, particularly in chapter 3? Is calling something "irreducible" a way of thumbing one's nose at the scientific framework, of saying, "Aha! Here is something you will never explain!"? To put the matter this way, in terms of a kind of stand-off between the supposedly "reductionist" ambitions of science and a supposedly recalcitrant domain related to the soul, is unhelpful and misleading. For the scientific enterprise is a complex and multifaceted endeavour, and to see it as feeding all phenomena into a monolithic reductive mill seems something of a caricature. Few biologists, for example, would say that the living things they study, and the structures that explain them, are "reducible" in any straightforward sense to chemical or physical phenomena, or to be unravelled in terms of a single style of explanatory template.

In the light of these drawbacks to talking about "irreducibility," let us see whether another concept often used in this kind of context fares any better—namely, the notion of *transcendence*. If we look at the etymological connotations of the Latin root from which it is derived, to *transcend* is to climb across or beyond a barrier, or to exceed some boundary. So to talk of something as being transcendent in the present context seems to carry the implication that it is outside or beyond the boundaries of scientific investigation. But in order to see just what might count as "transcendent" in this sense, we need to distinguish two dimensions of transcendence: a subjective dimension, relating to the phenomenon of individual conscious experience, and an objective dimension, relating to the reality that is thereby experienced.

Let us take the subjective dimension first. Do you and I, in virtue of our status as subjective centres of awareness—"this *me*, that is to say the soul, by which I am what I am"—somehow qualify as "transcendent" beings, individuals whose mode of being lies "outside" the physical domain or "beyond" the phenomena studied by science? To put the matter this way seems problematic, if only because it can easily incline us to construe the soul as a "strange" or "spooky" kind of entity, a supernatural or immaterial object existing in a different realm from anything that could be investigated by science. Yet as should be clear from looking back at our earlier discussion of the nature of the soul in chapter 2, an examination of the way in which "soul" has been understood by philosophers by no means licenses the conclusion that an immaterialist view of the soul is the only possible, or even the most plausible, conception.

From a present-day perspective, the cumulative lesson that emerges from the long history of philosophical wrestling with the concept of the soul, together with the increasing fertility of scientific research into the physiological underpinnings of mental functioning, is that the notion of soul as immaterial substance has, for most people, ceased to discharge a useful explanatory function, even assuming that it once did so (which is doubtful, since calling the soul an immaterial thing gets us no nearer to understanding how it exercises its functions). Some may wish to discard the immaterialist conception altogether, while others may prefer to remain agnostic about whether such substances exist, and yet others may feel they have to hold on to it for religious, and in particular theistic, reasons. But on this last point, it is by no means clear that belief in a personal God requires us to favour Descartes over Aristotle, and suppose that being human involves the existence of a soul in the sense of a Cartesian-style immaterial substance, as opposed to construing it along Aristotelian or "hylemorphic" lines as the form of the body.[2] If we follow something like this latter view, all the precious properties and capacities that we group under the heading of "soul," and which we rightly value as indispensable to our humanity—our powers of thought and feeling, our imaginative and emotional powers, our capacity for profound and transformative spiritual experience—all these could be powers that we humans possess in virtue of our *embodiment*, in virtue of our existence as a biological species of a certain kind, operating in a complex social environment and possessed of brains and nervous systems configured in such a way as to allow us to engage in the whole rich repertoire of functions and activities just mentioned. Humans, we can say, do indeed have souls in this attributive sense: our world view needs to make room for the soul, insofar as that notion refers to our possession of all these rich capacities and activities without which we would not be properly human. But for those who believe in a personal creator God, it is hard to see how the creation of human beings need require God to create immaterial substances, *in addition* to creating the complex biological creatures that we are, physically configured in such a way as to have all the powers and capacities in question.

Yet even if the attributes of soul are rooted in suitably configured matter, there remains something about the subjective dimension of experience that is *sui generis*, in a unique category of its own. The sculptor Antony Gormley once reflected in an interview on the experience of shutting one's eyes and feeling enclosed within the body, like the dark room in which he was sometimes locked up as a little boy: utterly hemmed in and yet somehow inhabiting an *infinite space*, like the infinite space of

2. See ch. 2, "Out of This World?"

the cosmos.[3] As human beings we know we are limited, confined within the constraints of a biological body that is mortal and finite, inhabiting a tiny temporary speck of the vast cosmos. Scientific understanding can track the history of this tiny biological creature, investigate its workings, map its brain activity, trace out its behaviour from conception to death. And yet none of this scientific mapping unlocks the domain of subjective conscious awareness, that fragile and fleeting private space that each of us inhabits when we close our eyes and hear the pulse of our thoughts and feelings and sensations—fragile, fleeting, transient, wholly finite, yet ranging out to the infinite world of which, while it endures, it remains, mysteriously, the subject and the centre. There is a kind of transcendence here, one that has nothing to do with immaterial souls or disembodied spirits, but which is rooted in something none of us can deny, our own conscious presence in the world as enduring centres of awareness, and graspers of meaning and value.

But when the individual subject reaches out and encounters a world of meaning and value, then sooner or later it is drawn to reflect on the second of the two dimensions of transcendence referred to above, the objective dimension. Our world picture needs not just to make room for us humans, and the "soul qualities" that give us individual conscious awareness as subjects of experience, but also to make room for the *reality of what we apprehend* when we exercise those qualities. That within us which we call the "soul," though it may not be a "thing," still less an immaterial thing, can thus be thought of as an *instrument of transcendence*.[4] It is an instrument that allows

3. In the film *Being Human*, directed by Morag Tinto for the BBC, 2015.

4. See Thomas Nagel: "Consciousness [is] an instrument of transcendence that can grasp objective reality and objective value" (*Mind and Cosmos*, 85).

us access to the timeless truths of logic and mathematics and the timeless authoritative power of values that we are constrained to recognize and acknowledge whether we like it or not. And in moments of heightened awareness, it allows us to see through the confused morass of our contingent appetites and desires, past the imperatives of survival and all the day-to-day demands that surround us, towards an objective and timeless good that calls us to reach forward to what we are not yet, but which we somehow aspire to be. We may ourselves be finite, corporeal, mortal, imperfect, yet we cannot easily deny that we feel the pull of that transcendent goodness. As Augustine and Bonaventure and Descartes all saw, it is of the nature of a finite creature to reach towards the infinite—something it cannot fully grasp, but which it somehow apprehends even in the very awareness of its own finitude.[5]

Natural versus Supernatural: The Unhelpful Contrast

In reflecting, as we have just been doing, on the soul as an "instrument of transcendence," we began with the subjective domain of individual conscious awareness and moved on to the objective reality accessed in virtue of that awareness. Much of that reality involves a widely acknowledged domain of meaning and value, recognized and accepted from a variety of philosophical perspectives including purely secular ones, though there may be fierce philosophical disagreements about its status and its ultimate grounding. But by the end of the previous section, our reflections on the transcendent arrived at something much

---

5. See Cottingham, "From Desire to Encounter."

more controversial, the idea of what might be called the transcendent with a capital "T"—the infinite source of being and goodness that is the object of theistic belief. Some, of course, will entirely reject this final step, and it is no part of the aim of this book to offer a demonstrative or probabilistic proof of its validity. Philosophical discourse, so it seems to me, is seldom if ever a matter of coercive argument, but has more to do with trying to show how certain frameworks of interpretation are hospitable to coming to terms with the existential and moral challenges inherent in our human predicament.

But irrespective of whether we are prepared to make the final step towards the transcendent with a capital "T," it is important to be clear about how this notion of the transcendent relates to another term so often found in discussions of religious belief— namely, the *supernatural*. There is no doubt that one of the main reasons why many people reject religious belief is that they find the whole idea of a supernatural domain untenable, or even absurd. And among those on the other side who are believers, it seems likely that a survey would show that many consider their faith to be bound up with accepting the idea of supernatural entities, powers, or forces. The point is not unrelated to the discussion in the previous section of whether what is called the soul in human beings can be understood as a set of biologically grounded attributes and capacities, as opposed to an immaterial substance. For one suspects that behind the strong resistance felt by some believers to giving up the idea of an immaterial soul in the human case is the implicit fear that once we allow the attributes of the soul to be biologically underpinned, rooted in biological structures, we may be on the way to saying that *all* reality must be rooted in physical structures, and so may be on the way to an atheistic world picture. For does not the theistic framework itself necessarily commit us to an immaterial or supernatural realm? Is not God supposed to be a supernatural being?

It cannot be denied that a great deal of writing on religious belief has focused on the idea of belief in a supernatural domain. And certainly, calling God "supernatural" can perhaps usefully serve to flag up the role of God as transcendent creator, not reducible to the physical universe, or to be identified with the natural world, as in pantheism. That granted, it nevertheless seems to me that on balance the term "supernatural" turns out to be more of a hindrance than a help when it comes to explicating what is involved in holding a theistic outlook. In the first place, it may invite us to "locate" God *outside* the natural world, as if there are two worlds, and two kinds of being—those that dwell here in the physical cosmos and those that dwell in "another place," perhaps visiting our universe from time to time. That is of course a crude caricature, but as so often when we are dealing not with empirical hypotheses but with metaphysical frameworks of interpretation, a certain image may hold us captive, even though when challenged we would say that "of course we did not quite mean *that*." It is very easy, as Nicolas Malebranche warned in the seventeenth century (following the much earlier lead of Aquinas), to "humanize" God—to construe him as a kind of entity in addition to those we know of already, but then to add that he is an entity of a supernatural kind. Even when, following Scripture, we call God a "mind" or "spirit," warns Malebranche, we should use such language not so much to show positively what God is as to indicate that he is not material. And even this is not quite right, since the infinite God must:

> contain within him the perfections of matter while not being material, just as he includes the perfections of created minds

without being a mind in the way we conceive of minds. His true name is HE WHO IS, i.e. unrestricted being, all being, the infinite and universal being.[6]

The idea of God as the infinite source of being who contains within himself the perfections of matter and of mind points to the traditional idea that all created things bear in some way the stamp of the divine, albeit in some cases very remotely and indistinctly.[7] This provides a further reason why the term "supernatural" can be unhelpful—namely, that it risks removing God from the world we know, the very world that is our principal means of access to the divine.

Just as we cannot properly understand the soul if we construe it in isolation from our experience as embodied creatures living in the world, so we cannot begin to approach the notion of the divine if we construe it in isolation from what is made manifest in the natural world around us. This consideration is of a piece with various movements in religious thought that emphasize the *immanence* of God rather than his transcendence. One thinks here of interest in recent years, in the theology of *panentheism* (as contrasted with pantheism); this resists baldly identifying God with the world in a pantheistic way, but nevertheless stresses the divine presence in all things.[8] In his 1984–85 Gifford Lectures entitled *God in Creation*, we find the German theologian Jürgen Moltmann saying the following:

6. Malebranche, *Search after Truth*, bk. 3, pt. 2, ch. 9, 251.

7. See Descartes, *Conversation with Burman* [1648], 17, AT, vol. 5, 156; CSMK, 340.

8. See Clayton, *Problem of God*. See also Yitzhak Melamed: pantheism asserts a "*symmetric* dependence between God and the world of finite things," so that "the world is in God and God is in the world," while panentheism "asserts an *asymmetric* dependence," so that all of nature, all the bodies (and thoughts) comprising the world, are "in God," yet "do not exhaust God"—"Cohen, Spinoza," 4, emphasis added.

God is not merely the Creator of the world. He is also the Spirit of the universe. Through the powers and potentialities of the Spirit, the Creator *indwells* the creatures he has made, animates them, holds them in life, and leads them into the future of his kingdom.[9]

Moltmann goes on to reject the idea of an "antithesis between God and the world" that defines God and the world "over against one another [so that] God is not-worldly and the world not divine."[10] As theological support for this, he cites the Jewish doctrine of *Shekinah*—the idea of the "descent of God to human beings and his dwelling among them,"[11] and also the Christian doctrine of the Trinity, where "through the power of the Spirit God is himself present in his creation—present in his reconciliation and his redemption of that creation."[12] This does not mean denying the traditional idea of the transcendence of God; but in mainstream theology, God's immanence and his transcendence go hand in hand, as it were, like two faces of the same coin; as the American writer Brad Gregory has put it, divine transcendence is "not the opposite but the *correlate* of divine immanence."[13]

The idea of the divine as manifest in the world, of nature as "charged with the grandeur of God," as Gerard Manley Hopkins expresses it, and as present within each human soul, "closer to me than I am to myself," as Augustine put it,[14] or as he "in whom

9. Moltmann, *God in Creation*, 14.

10. Moltmann, *God in Creation*, 14–15. See further Ellis, *God, Value, and Nature*.

11. Rosenzweig, *Star of Redemption*, pt. 3, bk. 3, 192; cited in Moltmann, *God in Creation*, 11.

12. Moltmann, *God in Creation*, 150.

13. Gregory, "No Room for God," 503; cited in Ellis, *God, Value, and Nature*, 151.

14. "*Interior intimo meo*": Augustine, *Confessions*, bk. 3, ch. 6, sec. 11.

we live and move and have our being," as St Paul put it much earlier[15]—these important notions further erode the usefulness of the classification "supernatural" as applied to that which we call God. To be sure, if we buy into the modern image of the natural world as "disenchanted," void of meaning and value,[16] then there will be little choice but to look "beyond" nature and the natural when we are trying to accommodate our intimations of the divine. But there is a long-standing and much richer conception of nature that flourished for many centuries before the contemporary secularized notion of the "natural" took hold, and if we cast an eye back to that earlier conception we find that much of the motivation behind the insistence on introducing the term "supernatural" in connection with religious experience starts to ebb away.

If we go back to Aristotle, his term *physis* denotes the world of physical nature; and in some respects, to be sure, as in his concepts of efficient and material causation, Aristotelian physics has something in common with the mechanistic approach of his corpuscularian predecessors, such as Democritus, and indeed with elements of modern physics. But to fully understand the term *physis* in Aristotle one has to see it through the lens of his teleological vision of the cosmos. Nature, in this sense, "does nothing in vain," as Aristotle famously asserts;[17] or as Leibniz put it much later, reviving and indeed radically updating the Aristotelian notion to fit a Christian context, the "divine and infinitely marvellous artifice of the Author of nature [ensures] . . . there is nothing waste, nothing sterile,

15. Acts 17:28.

16. See above, ch. 1, "Dimensions of Soul."

17. For example, in *De caelo*, ch. 1, sec. 4; *De partibus animalium*, ch. 2, sec. 13. For more on this theme in Aristotle, see R. J. Hankinson, "Philosophy of Science."

nothing dead in the universe; no chaos, no confusions, save in appearance."[18]

To take another important example, Descartes, normally thought of as poles apart from Aristotle and Leibniz in taking a distinctly non-normative and mechanistic view of the natural world, often in fact uses "nature" in a strongly normative sense. The closing section of Descartes's *Meditations* contains three successive paragraphs all beginning with the phrase "*Natura docet*"—"nature teaches."[19] The things that nature teaches seem at first to be the things we are often spontaneously inclined to believe—such as that the stars are very small, or that the Earth is immobile and flat. But these, Descartes goes on to insist, are only the *apparent* teachings of nature—rash beliefs that were acquired by the "natural" (in one sense) human habit of jumping to conclusions. It emerges by the close of the *Meditations* that the true teachings of nature come from Nature in a much grander sense: "I understand by the term *none other than God himself, or the order and disposition established by God in created things* . . . [or, in the case of my own nature] the totality of things bestowed on me by God."[20] What we are "naturally" inclined to believe, in the mundane factual sense of "natural"—what we often as a matter of fact tend to believe—has no authority at all; indeed it is a major purpose of the Cartesian programme to rid ourselves of the preconceived opinions acquired through unthinking habit or prejudice. But what we are inclined, indeed spontaneously impelled, to believe when the "natural light," the *lumen naturale*, illumines our minds is nothing else but the

18. Leibniz, *Monadology*, para. 69.

19. For more on this, see Cottingham, "Descartes, Sixth Meditation."

20. Descartes, *Meditations*, Sixth Meditation, AT, vol. 7, 80; CSM, vol. 2, 56; emphasis added.

deliverances of the divinely implanted faculty of reason—what Descartes elsewhere called the *lux rationis*.[21] Descartes's conception of nature here is as normative as could be.

So both nature as a whole and our own human nature (when properly and attentively used) must be understood (according to Descartes) as not just a matter of brute fact but as somehow authoritative. Coming down to the eighteenth century, we see these normative connotations of "nature" and "natural" still very much in evidence. For example, Joseph Butler speaks of conscience as "our *natural* guide, the guide assigned us by the Author of our nature"; and he goes on to say that "it therefore belongs to our condition of being, it is our duty, to walk in that path and follow this guide."[22] And by the end of the eighteenth century, with the rise of Romanticism, we find William Wordsworth celebrating the guiding role not just of our own human nature and the voice of conscience within us, but also of nature in the wider sense of the natural world around us, whose beauty and goodness speak to us and inspire us. In the poem we have had occasion to refer to earlier, his "Lines Composed a Few Miles above Tintern Abbey" (composed in 1798, some seventy years after Joseph Butler penned his *Sermons*), the notion of nature as a leader or guide is particularly prominent:

> Nature never did betray
> The heart that loved her; 'tis her privilege
> Through all the years of this our life, to lead
> From joy to joy . . .[23]

21. The notion of *lux rationis*, or "the light of reason," is found in Descartes, *Rules*, AT, vol. 10, 368; CSM, vol. 1, 14; in the *Meditations* it becomes the *lumen naturale*, the "natural light" (e.g., AT, vol. 7, 40; CSM, vol. 2, 28).

22. Butler, *Fifteen Sermons*, sermon 3, 5; emphasis added.

23. Wordsworth, "Tintern Abbey," lines 123–26.

Nature here has a specific role—to guide us throughout the allotted span of our mortal lives to experiences that will put us in touch with a deeper moral and aesthetic reality that infuses the world around us. In saying that this is Nature's "privilege," Wordsworth is not just referring to an effect that, at the purely empirical level, the natural environment has upon us; rather nature has a role that finds a place with the overall providential scheme of things. The language here is inescapably teleological: though Wordsworth does not make it explicit, Nature is in this sense the "handmaid" of the Author of Nature—she has been given a privileged job to do, to attend to the development of the moral sensibility of humankind.

A striking feature of the examples I have been citing, from classical times down to the early-modern epoch and later, is that there is very little if any use of the term *supernatural*. In Descartes, for instance, although when challenged he dutifully declared his allegiance to the "supernatural light" of faith,[24] in the many other places where he discusses our capacity to be guided towards truth and goodness he always construes it as part of our natural endowment, part of "the order and disposition established by God in created things."[25] For all three of the authors just mentioned, it is *in the natural world* that God's presence is manifest—for Descartes, in the divinely ordained realities apprehended via the natural light of reason; for Butler, in the authoritative requirements disclosed to us through the workings of conscience; for Wordsworth, in the beauties of the natural world that we joyfully acknowledge as "full of blessings."[26] What one might call the "operativeness" of the divine, in all

24. Descartes, *Meditations*, Second Replies, AT, vol. 7, 148; CSM, vol. 2, 106.
25. Descartes, *Meditations*, Sixth Meditation, AT, vol. 7, 80; CSM, vol. 2, 56.
26. Wordsworth, "Tintern Abbey," line 136.

these cases is immanent in the natural order of things. The created order, including both the natural world around us and our own nature, is configured by God, irradiated with the divine. The picture of reality that emerges from all this, both as regards the human attributes and capacities traditionally assigned to the human "soul" and as regards the wondrous realities we encounter when these human powers are activated, invites us not so much to speculate about an "other-worldly" supernatural domain as to reflect on the mystery and wonder of the "Nature" of which we are privileged to be a part.[27]

Immortal Longings and the Care of the Soul: From Metaphysics to Praxis

Largely absent from our discussion so far has been a recurrent theme in religious and philosophical thinking about the soul—namely, the idea of the soul as immortal. Certainly many religious believers are committed to this notion: it is prominent in Christianity and Islam, though on balance less so in Judaism. And, as we saw in chapter 2, there is a philosophical tradition going back to Plato that takes the immortality of the soul to be a consequence of its supposedly immaterial or non-bodily nature.[28]

Plato's argument for this linkage between immateriality and immortality is, it has to be said, far from convincing. As Descartes acknowledged many centuries later, there is no logical guarantee that an immaterial substance will continue in existence after the death of the body—it might, for all we know,

---

27. See further Fiona Ellis's discussion of enriched or "expansive" naturalism, in her *God, Value, and Nature*.

28. See above, ch. 2, "Out of This World?"

just peter out and cease to be when the body is destroyed.[29] It is perhaps worth adding, conversely, that materiality need not necessarily imply mortality. If the soul is *not* an immaterial substance but (along Aristotelian lines) a principle whereby material structures are configured so as to allow faculties such as perception and thought to operate,[30] then it still seems theoretically possible that such faculties could be reactivated in some kind of "new body" after the death of this earthly biological body. This appears to have been St Paul's conception, when he declared that in the resurrection, what was sown as a *soma psychikon* (biological body) would be raised as a different kind of body, a *soma pneumatikon* (spiritual body).[31]

For those with a taste for metaphysical speculations, there are unending labyrinths of argument that could be entered into here. But in line with the general strategy followed in much of this book, it will be more fruitful for our purposes to focus on how these questions bear on the human predicament that each of us faces as we confront the problems of our existence. One does not have to go along with all the conclusions of the pragmatist philosophers in order to see some virtue in the basic claim of pragmatism that, as William James put it, "you must bring out of each word its practical cash-value, and set it in the stream of your experience."[32] We saw in the previous section, with respect to the term "supernatural," that explicating theistic belief in terms of belief in a domain set over against the natural realm may be less helpful than uncovering how the theistic

29. Descartes, *Meditations*, Second Replies, AT, vol. 7, 153; CSM, vol. 2, 109. This possible objection had in fact been raised by Plato himself, in the mouthpiece of "Cebes" (*Phaedo*, 77b–c).

30. See above, ch. 2, "Out of This World?"

31. 1 Corinthians 15:44.

32. James, *Pragmatism*, 28.

outlook informs our conception of ourselves and the natural world we inhabit. Something similar may apply in the case of the traditional doctrine of the soul's immortality. If we look at the practical implications of that doctrine, as it figures in religious writings and forms of life, we find it is strongly connected with two ideas.

The first is that of *meaning*. What Charles Taylor has called the "serious . . . unstillable longing" for immortality within the human spirit is linked to the hope that the significance of our lives, and perhaps most crucially the lives of those we love who have died, is somehow "gathered in," and hence that these lives ultimately amount to something more than a series of events and actions irreversible and finally terminated in death. In Taylor's analysis, the loss of this hope in an eternal dimension of meaning has led to "a sense of void . . . and of deep embarrassment" in the way the phenomenon of death is handled in our contemporary secular culture.[33] Whether human beings in a wholly secularized culture could learn to live with this void without succumbing to a sense of futility remains to be seen.

The second idea that has been closely associated with the concept of the soul's immortality is the idea of personal *accountability*—the idea that all our actions in this life have ultimate moral significance, that they remain for ever subject to judgement and cannot simply be swept away and forgotten through the erosions of time.[34] In this context, having a soul involves above all being a moral agent and having rational and emotional capacities that allow us to act well or badly, to treat

33. Taylor, *Secular Age*, 720, 722.
34. See, for example, the story of the last judgement in Matthew 25:31–46. The most famous philosophical treatment of the connection between soul or self and accountability is in Locke, *Essay Concerning Human Understanding*, bk. 2, ch. 27.

our fellow creatures with love and respect, or, alternatively, to treat them as either not worthy of serious attention, or, possibly even worse, simply as a means to our own gratification or convenience. The idea of the soul's immortality, and of an eternal judge of supreme power and love to whom we must render an account of ourselves, and before whom none of the secrets of our souls are hidden, encapsulates the idea that how we use our moral agency ultimately matters. But that "mattering," on a theistic view, is not just the self-interested question of whether we shall be rewarded or punished in some future existence. It recapitulates instead the idea explored in earlier chapters that at the heart of reality are normative demands that *confront* us, that we cannot escape, try as we might,[35] and that these demands retain their power and authority irrespective of how the actual consequences of our actions actually pan out during our lifespan on Earth.

In one of the many scriptural passages in which the word "soul" appears are these lines from the Psalms:

> My heart is not proud; my eyes are not raised too high;
>   I do not occupy myself with matters too marvellous
>   for me.
> But I have calmed and quieted my soul, like a weaned
>   child with its mother; like a weaned child is my soul
>   within me.[36]

The Psalm is in part an expression of humility. But in the context of our present discussion, it could also be interpreted as a resolve to forswear metaphysical speculations (matters too "high" and "marvellous") in favour of more practical human

---

35. See above, ch. 3, "The Domain of the Soul."
36. Psalm 131:1–2.

concerns, such as the longing of the restless mind for calm. But the "calmness of soul" of which the verses speak is not just something anodyne and tranquillizing. It depends, as the third and concluding verse of this very short Psalm goes on to make clear, on the right relation to God, a relation of trustful hope.[37] And clearly that relation of calm hope can only exist if all is well within the soul—in other words, if the demands of righteousness have not been violated.

This brings us back to the theme first broached in our opening chapter, the "care of the soul," understood by Socrates in terms of right conduct, caring for the things that matter, as opposed to the material gratifications of wealth and personal gain.[38] Of course this overriding care for the conduct of life, for what might be called the soul as moral agenthood, does not have to be expressed in religious terms. And it is obvious that someone can be an exemplary human being, be adept at "caring for the soul" in the sense now under discussion, without having any theistic allegiance. But what the theistic framework adds to this is the sense of "existing before God," in Kierkegaard's phrase.[39] This is the sense that a good and acceptable life is not just a collection of good acts by the agent, nor even the cultivation of ingrained habits of conduct that predispose one to make the right choices and have the right feelings. More than that, it is the sense, described earlier, that a human life has ultimate significance, and has to be presented to God like an offering (to use a Pauline notion).[40] In this overriding task of human life, it is important, given the kinds of being humans are, that we do

37. "O Israel trust in the Lord; both now and evermore." Psalm 131:3.
38. See above, ch. 1, "The Risk of Loss."
39. See above, ch. 1, "The Risk of Loss."
40. Romans 12:1.

not indulge the rationalistic fantasy of assuming we can map out the conditions for the good life using the tools of "practical reason."[41] That, to be sure, will be part of the story; but we will also need to address the task not with "left-brain" skills alone,[42] but using all the resources of the human psyche.

Highly relevant in this context is the fact that religious allegiance is not just a matter of adopting a belief system, but involves entering a "form of life," a structured system of practices, individual and collective, which will enact and reinforce our commitment to the good and the care of our souls. For we human beings need, in order to flourish, not just to act rightly, not just to exercise our "practical reason" or "rational choice," but to have acquired and thoroughly absorbed a conception of goodness that guides and irradiates our lives. And this requires people, as the distinguished philosopher Robert Adams has argued, to have outward ways of *expressing their allegiance to the good*:

> Something of ethical importance can be done in worship that we cannot accomplish except symbolically. . . . Getting ourselves dressed in the morning, [going] to work, and then home again to dinner, we try on the way and in between to do some good, to love people and be kind to them, to enjoy and perhaps to create some beauty. But none of this

41. See above, ch. 4, "The Depths of the Psyche."

42. For the notion of two modes of awareness, corresponding to the two hemispheres of the brain, see the seminal work of Iain McGilchrist, *Master and His Emissary*, esp. 93. It should be added that associating these two modes of awareness with the right and left hemispheres, respectively, is something of a schematic approximation, as McGilchrist himself stresses. There is evidence to suggest that in most people the respective functions do broadly correlate with neural activity in the relevant halves of the brain, but in normal subjects there is constant interaction between the halves.

is very perfect, even when we succeed; and all of it is very fragmentary. . . . Symbolically, we can do better. Symbolically I can be for the Good as such, and not just for the bits and pieces of it that I can concretely promote. . . . I can be for the good by articulating or accepting some conception of a comprehensive and perfect or transcendent Good and expressing my loyalty to it symbolically. . . . The symbolism provides something for which there is no adequate substitute. Theists find this value of symbolism supremely in worship.[43]

Worship thus enacts a special kind of "care for the soul," a kind of care that not only attempts to enact and make explicit our being "for the good," in the way described by Adams, but which also gives vivid symbolic expression to the hidden longings of the soul described at the end of the previous chapter and the start of the present—the longing of the finite creature for transcendence. Sacramental worship may be thought of as a process whereby the finite creature *enacts* the search for the infinite perfection that it cannot fully grasp. In the Mass or the Eucharist that is at the centre of much Christian worship, those who participate orient themselves, through liturgical practice and ritual, towards that for which they long. Thus the drama of the Mass begins with a *journey*: in the opening antiphon, the priest intones "*Introibo ad altare Dei*" (I will go up to the altar of God)—note the future tense—which is a quotation from Psalm 43:4, a song of longing to be "brought up to the holy mountain of God," and this is embodied in ritual as the celebrant processes up the altar steps.

What is expressed in all this, and in many other related spiritual practices and rituals, is the longing of the finite creature for

43. Adams, *Finite and Infinite Goods*, 227.

communion with the infinite—that which cannot be compre-hended, cannot be grasped, but whose presence no atheist or secularist is in a position to deny, nor to condemn the search for it as hopeless and irrational. For what cannot be compre-hended can nevertheless be glimpsed, through the transforma-tions worked by spiritual praxis. It is glimpsed as holy—holy (as Emmanuel Levinas might put it) in its *otherness*, as the un-reachable object of our longing, but also holy in the awe it calls forth as the sacred source of normativity—precisely that ines-capable summons that Levinas identifies us as experiencing in our encounters with our fellow creatures.[44] By enacting our human longing for the good, and expressing our responsiveness to it, spiritual praxis embodies and constitutes our engagement with the divine, and enables the human soul to encounter, insofar as its finitude allows, the infinite perfection that passes all understanding.[45]

Transcendence and Our Human Destiny

Friedrich Nietzsche, famous for proclaiming the death of God, is sometimes seen as one of the founding fathers of con-temporary atheism, but one does not have to delve very far into his writings in order to see that his outlook has little in common with that of the militant atheists of our own time. On the con-trary, there is a good case for saying that he had a profoundly religious sensibility. The "death of God," the collapse of religion, is something he foresees, but which he warns of with grim fore-boding: he sees it as coinciding with the collapse of humanity itself—the end of *being human* as we now understand it. His

44. Levinas, "Beyond Intentionality."
45. See further Cottingham, "Engagement, Immersion and Enactment."

mouthpiece Zarathustra prophesies that the grim time is coming when "the soil of our culture will be poor and exhausted so that nothing will grow." This will be the time of "that most contemptible creature, the last man." Why contemptible, why the last man? Because from then on man will "no longer launch the arrow of his longing beyond man."[46] Or in the words of an earlier work, the *Untimely Meditations*, the human being will have lost the yearning to "be consecrated to something higher than itself."[47] Humanity will have ceased to reach for the transcendent.[48]

The philosophical temptation is always to classify the transcendent. If this means to give a positive characterization in literal language, such an undertaking is impossible. That which is dimly apprehended as the direction towards which the "arrow of our longing" points is, as mainstream theology has always asserted, beyond explicit human comprehension;[49] it is like the mountain that we cannot grasp, cannot put our arms around, but which we can nevertheless somehow reach towards.[50] Yet we know at least that the reality towards which we reach cannot be a wholly abstract or impersonal one, for how could something abstract and impersonal exert an authoritative, normative pull upon us, call us forward to transcend our weakness and failure and become something better? That transcendent reality, for the theist, is the unknown source of truth and goodness that, in the words of Aquinas, "everyone calls God."[51] And in

46. Nietzsche, *Thus Spake Zarathustra*, pt. 1, Zarathustra's prologue, 169. See further Gemes, "Postmodernism's Use."

47. Nietzsche, *Untimely Meditations*, essay 4, sec. 4, 212.

48. Cf. Karl Rahner, quoted above, ch. 4, "The Depths of the Psyche."

49. Aquinas, *Summa theologiae*, pt. 1, qu. 12, art. 7.

50. Descartes, letter to Mersenne, 27 May 1630, AT, vol. 1, 152; CSMK, 25.

51. Aquinas, *Summa theologiae*, pt. 1, qu. 2, art. 3.

virtue of those capacities we refer to by the label "soul," we are indeed able to glimpse something of that reality. As the Jewish spiritual writer Wayne Dosick has put it:

> That which makes . . . a person capable of thinking and knowing, reasoning and remembering, a person capable of doing justly and feeling compassion—is the soul. And the human soul is a tiny piece of God, a tiny fragment of God's light, a spark of the Divine that burst forth from the heavenly vessels and showered the universe.[52]

Many writers trying to grapple with this have had recourse to metaphor. And as has been implicitly or explicitly suggested in many places throughout this book, it would be a mistake to insist that there is something philosophically unsatisfactory about this, since philosophical understanding cannot be achieved by the abstract analysis of the intellect alone, but requires all the resources of the human psyche.[53] The metaphor of light as a symbol of the divine has a long history in spiritual and indeed philosophical writings,[54] partly because it has a double import, indicating both an outer dimension, the stream of energy that is a pervasive feature of the universe, giving substance and visibility to the whole natural world, and also an inner dimension, in the illumination of human consciousness that enables us to glimpse and respond to that reality.

So in virtue of that "spark of the divine" that Dosick identifies with the human soul, there is a kind of affinity between the

---

52. Dosick, *Living Judaism*, 2.

53. See, for instance, ch. 1, "Dimensions of Soul"; ch 4, "The Soul's Hidden Yearning for God." See further Cottingham, *Philosophy of Religion*, ch. 1.

54. The metaphor has its philosophical origins in Plato (*Republic*, bk. 5); its most famous scriptural appearance is in the first chapter of St. John's Gospel.

ultimate reality that underlies the cosmos and the way our own minds are configured. It would be easy for the modern sceptic to dismiss this as a fanciful idea, but the idea certainly has a physical parallel or analogue insofar as science has revealed that we humans are indeed fragments of stardust, our bodies configured and moulded out of the very elements cast forth billions of years ago from an exploding star. To be willing to use the terminology of the divinely illuminated soul in understanding our human nature is in effect to say that just as our physical and biological nature has cosmic origins, so too our destiny, the goal we glimpse and towards which we must orient ourselves in order to find fulfilment, arises from a cosmic teleology.

The poet Wordsworth spoke of "the soul that rises with us, our life's star," and saw us as entering the world "trailing clouds of glory from God, who is our home"—the source of being and goodness to which we are destined to return.[55] The language is quasi-Platonic, evoking Plato's idea of the soul as endowed with innate knowledge that it "recollects" from a former existence.[56] But Wordsworth is less interested in metaphysics than in the moral and spiritual dimensions of soul that we have been reflecting on so frequently throughout this book. What is most important about these dimensions does not have to be expressed in terms of elaborate theological theories or doctrines. The crucial point is that in virtue of our human capacities of "soul," we humans have a strong and vivid intimation of the power of goodness, a power that transcends the muddle and decay of so much of our human existence, and points us towards

55. Wordsworth, "Ode: Intimations of Immortality," lines 64–65, in *Critical Edition*, 299.

56. Plato, *Phaedo* 73–74; *Meno* 84–85.

our true destiny—accomplishing the task of "finding the soul," of realizing the better selves we are meant to be.

This inescapable teleological vision has some affinities with the ancient philosophical concept discussed in the third section of chapter 1 (*The Soul and Human Nature*), namely the Aristotelian idea of a *telos*, a goal laid down for human existence, and linked to our very essence as human beings. To hold on to the idea of the soul in this context is to hold on to the idea of an objective teleological framework for human life. In its theistic form, this framework is held to be objective in the strongest possible sense: the teleology is, as it were, a cosmic one, written into the ultimate nature of reality, stemming from the transcendent source of all being and goodness. But what hope can there be of holding on to such a vision in our modern age? Many philosophers would say there is no hope whatsoever. So we find Bernard Williams firmly closing the door to such a hope when he insists that "the first and hardest lesson of Darwinism, [is] that there is no such teleology at all, and that there is no orchestral score provided from anywhere according to which human beings have a special part to play."[57]

Certainly, anyone maintaining that the complete totality of nature is in any sense divine or divinely infused has to face the distinct implausibility of the belief in an inherent trend or flow in nature towards improvement and perfection. The natural world is a mixture, providing beauty and wonder, but also terrible destruction and devastation, catastrophic waste and inexorable decay. If there is an unfolding process here, there seems no persuasive argument for construing it as intrinsically ordered towards either physical or moral amelioration. To

57. Williams, *Making Sense of Humanity*, 109–10. The importance of this passage is well brought out in McPherson, "Cosmic Outlooks."

suppose otherwise can seem like the fallacy so prevalent in the nineteenth century when inexhaustible growth and economic progress seemed to beckon. With hindsight, after the carnage of the twentieth century, and our insane greed that is, perhaps irreversibly, degrading the biosphere in the twenty-first, we now know, or should know, better. In the actual empirical facts of how the world behaves, and of how we behave as part of that world, the balance sheet seems neutral or worse. If there is a direction here, it seems, so far from having divine status, to be more like the malign conative force that Schopenhauer discerned in nature, and which Thomas Hardy vividly invoked in the following stanzas from "The Convergence of the Twain," his beautiful but terrifying poem on the sinking of the *Titanic*. The passage begins with the building of this beautiful ship, the "creature of cleaving wing":

> Well: while was fashioning
> This creature of cleaving wing,
> The Immanent Will that stirs and urges everything
>
> Prepared a sinister mate
> For her—so gaily great—
> A Shape of Ice, for the time far and dissociate . . .
>
> Alien they seemed to be;
> No mortal eye could see
> The intimate welding of their later history . . .
>
> Till the Spinner of the Years
> Said "Now!" And each one hears,
> And consummation comes, and jars two hemispheres.[58]

58. Hardy, "The Convergence of the Twain" [1912], sts. 6, 7, 9, 11 in *Selected Poems*, 70; see further Brodsky, "Wooing the Inanimate."

The "Spinner of the Years" is of course not a transcendent deity but merely a poetic personification of the blind, Schopenhauerian immanent conatus. There is no redemption here, not even if some or many of the passengers on the doomed ship— perhaps those standing on the prow who imagine themselves in the Hegelian vanguard, as going with the flow, or representing its true direction—are busy exercising their "autonomous reason," or expressing their deepest love. For those on the prow, as for those below decks, the terrible consummation comes.

The trajectory of Hardy's *Titanic* may for present purposes be taken as a symbol for the direction of the universe as a whole, and of the planet Earth in particular, which there is good reason to regard as a doomed vessel, inexorably condemned by the laws of physics to incineration, with its remains, together with everything else, destined to end in final stasis in the entropic heatdeath of the cosmos. So to accept the theistic teleological framework cannot be, it seems, to believe in an actual causal direction to the unfolding of things. If there were this kind of "immanent teleology" in the universe, it would seem to have nothing to do with our needs, and thus would ultimately turn out to have no moral significance for us or our lives.[59] What is required to meet our human needs is a transcendent teleology, representing not the way the universe *is* going, but the way it *should* go, or, in human terms, the way we are called to be.

There are no doubt many ways in which human beings might try to come to terms with the gap between the actual, so often cruel and destructive, direction of the universe and the human longing to reach towards the good. Some are strategies of resignation, or of defiance, or of ironic detachment from the

59. See Nagel, *Secular Philosophy*, ch. 1; see also the "ananthropocentric purposivism" proposed by Tim Mulgan in *Purpose in the Universe*.

absurdity of it all. But in what is surely one of the hardest and yet most moving lessons offered by the theistic framework in its Christian form, the message is that even in the midst of cruelty and destructiveness, and without denying any of its horror, we are still called on to hold fast to the good, and to reach towards it in hope.

The task is fearfully difficult. But the care of the soul, within this framework, is nurtured and fostered by spiritual praxis, which is partly designed to encourage and support the weak and easily overwhelmed human quest for the transcendent. Many of the principal components in traditional theistic spiritual praxis, including adoration, confession, thanksgiving, and supplication, are directed to this end, aiming to orient us towards the glory that merits our joyful adoration, the normative standard against which we acknowledge our failure, the source and giver towards which we turn in thankfulness, and the loving recipient of our pleas for strength to endure.

To prove the existence of the object of our quest is beyond the capacity of the finite human intellect. But the human impulse to picture this object, and to describe it in metaphysical terms, persists. Wordsworth, as we have seen, spoke of it in Platonic fashion, and in the "Immortality Ode" quoted earlier he goes on to speak of how even in our earthbound existence the soul catches sight of the transcendent source from which it came:

> Hence in a season of calm weather,
> Though inland far we be
> Our souls have sight of that immortal sea
> Which brought us hither.[60]

---

60. Wordsworth, "Ode: Intimations of Immortality," lines 164–67.

The source of being and goodness is only glimpsed, though the intimations are strong. But the unquenchable yearnings of the human soul make it something like a spiritual imperative to believe in perfection beyond our imperfection, harmony beyond our strife, unchanging love beyond our vacillating desires, goodness beyond our flaws and failings. We need, in short, the transcendent. I suggested earlier that it is unhelpful to represent this God as dwelling in "another place," in a supernatural realm. Nor (in the wake of Kant's critical philosophy) does it seem likely that metaphysical speculation is going to yield anything in this area resembling discursive knowledge. But even if it surpasses our understanding, we need nevertheless to believe in the transcendent and to reach out to it in faith, hope, and love; metaphysics here has to give way to praxis. The transcendent dimension is something we must hold on to, or to borrow Kant's phrase, we must *will* that this not be taken from us;[61] for otherwise our deepest longings, which we cannot in integrity deny, would be in vain.

For the theist, this is the goal of our strivings, and in seeking it we hope to fulfil what is best in our nature, to realize our true selves, and thereby find meaning and completion. This, in the end, is the hoped-for destination to which the "quest for the soul" points. And in what can seem a paradox, or is maybe only another dimension of the mystery of our human nature, we engage in this "activity of the soul,"[62] and embark on this voyage of self-discovery and search for completion, in virtue of our embodiment. We may never slip the bonds of our physical nature, nor perhaps should we wish to, since our embodiment gives us our humanity, and brings us, weak and mortal though

61. "I firmly abide by this, and will not let this faith be taken from me;" Kant, *Critique of Practical Reason*, pt. 1, bk. 2, ch. 2, sec. 8.

62. See above, ch. 1, "The Soul and Human Nature."

we are, the immeasurable riches of conscious experience. But when we reach towards the transcendent, then the soul "soars enchanted,"[63] and, so far as our finite and imperfect nature allows, we rise "with silent lifting mind . . . and touch the face of God."[64]

63. See above, ch. 1, "Dimensions of Soul."

64. From the sonnet "High Flight" (1941) by John Gillespie Magee, lines 12 and 14. Text and facsimile of original manuscript in Haas, *Face of God*, front matter.

BIBLIOGRAPHY

Adams, Robert. *Finite and Infinite Goods*. Oxford: Oxford University Press, 1999.

Aquinas, Thomas. *Summa theologiae* [1266–73]. Translated by Fathers of the English Dominican Province. London: Burns, Oates and Washbourne, 1911.

Aristotle. *Categories* [c. 330 BCE]. Edited and translated by J. L. Ackrill. Oxford: Clarendon, 1963.

———. *De anima* [c. 325 BCE]. Edited and translated by D. W. Hamlyn. Oxford: Clarendon, 1968.

———. *De caelo* [c. 325 BCE]. Translated by J. L. Stocks. The Internet Classics Archive, by Daniel C. Stevenson, Web Atomics. http://classics.mit.edu/Aristotle/heavens.1.i.html.

———. *De partibus animalium*. Translated by W. Ogle. The Internet Classics Archive, by Daniel C. Stevenson, Web Atomics. http://classics.mit.edu/Aristotle/parts_animals.mb.txt.

———. *Eudemian Ethics* [c. 325 BCE]. Translated by A. Kenny. Oxford: Oxford World's Classics, 2011.

———. *Nicomachean Ethics* [c. 325 BCE]. Edited by T. Irwin. Indianapolis: Hackett, 1985.

Augustine of Hippo. *Confessions* [*Confessiones*; c. 398]. Translated by W. Watts. Cambridge, MA: Harvard University Press, 1912.

———. *De vera religione* [391]. In *Patrologia Latina*, edited by J. Migne, vol. 34, 123–72. Paris, 1857–66.

———. *Sermons* [*Sermones*; 392–430]. In *Patrologia Latina*, edited by J. Migne, vol. 38, 25–994. Paris, 1857–66.

Barnes, Jonathan, ed. *The Cambridge Companion to Aristotle*. Cambridge: Cambridge University Press, 1995.

Berkeley, George. *A Treatise Concerning the Principles of Human Knowledge* [1710]. Oxford: Oxford World's Classics, 1996.

Blackburn, Simon. *Essays in Quasi-Realism*. Oxford: Clarendon, 1993.

Bonaventure, St. *Itinerarium mentis in Deum* [Journey of the mind towards God; 1259]. Biblioteca Franciscana. [In Latin.] http://www.franciscanos.net/document/itinerl.htm. Translated by G. B. as "The Mind's Road to God" (Crossroads

Initiative, 28 January 2016, https://www.crossroadsinitiative.com/media/articles
/journey-of-the-mind-into-god/).

Brodsky, Joseph. "Wooing the Inanimate." In *On Grief and Reason*, 270–325. London: Penguin, 1996.

Butler, Joseph. *Fifteen Sermons* [1726]. In *British Moralists 1650–1800*, edited by D. D. Raphael, 325–386. Oxford: Clarendon, 1969.

Carlisle, Clare. *Kierkegaard's Fear and Trembling*. London: Continuum, 2010.

Chalmers, David. "Facing Up to the Problem of Consciousness." *Journal of Consciousness Studies* 2 (1995): 200–219.

Chen, Justin. "In Lofty Quest to Map Human Memories, a Scientist Journeys Deep into the Mind of a Worm." *STAT*. 13 August 2018. https://www.statnews.com /2018/08/13/connectome-neurology-mapping-cognition/?utm_source =STAT+Newsletters&utm_campaign=6a77ff852d-Daily_Recap&utm_medium =email&utm_term=0_8cab1d7961-6a77ff852d-150401685.

Chomsky, Noam. *Language and Mind*. New York: Harcourt, Brace and World, 1968.

Clayton, Philip. *The Problem of God in Modern Thought*. Grand Rapids, MI: Eerdmans, 2000.

Cottingham, John. "Cartesian Dualism: Theology, Metaphysics and Science." In *The Cambridge Companion to Descartes*, edited by Cottingham, 236–57. Cambridge: Cambridge University Press, 1992.

———. *Cartesian Reflections*. Oxford: Oxford University Press, 2008.

———. "Demandingness, Moral Development and Moral Philosophy." In *The Problem of Moral Demandingness*, edited by T. Chappell, 86–103. London: Palgrave, 2009.

———. *Descartes*. Oxford: Blackwell, 1986.

———. "Descartes and the Problem of Consciousness." In *Consciousness and the Great Philosophers: What Would They Have Said about Our Mind-Body Problem?* edited by S. Leach and J. Tartaglia, 63–72. London: Routledge, 2016.

———. "Descartes, Sixth Meditation: The External World, 'Nature' and Human Experience." In *Descartes's Meditations: Critical Essays*, edited by V. Chappell, 207–223. Lanham, MD: Rowman and Littlefield, 1997.

———. "Engagement, Immersion and Enactment: The Role of Spiritual Practice in Religious Belief." In *Philosophy and the Spiritual Life*, edited by V. Harrison. London: Routledge, forthcoming.

———. "From Desire to Encounter: The Human Quest for the Infinite." *Religious Studies* (2019) 55, 375–388.

———. "Happiness, Temporality, Meaning." In *Philosophy and Happiness*, edited by L. Bortolotti, 21–36. London: Palgrave, 2009.

———. "Integrity and Fragmentation." *Journal of Applied Philosophy* 27, no. 1 (2010): 2–14.

———. *On the Meaning of Life*. London: Routledge, 2003.

———. *Philosophy and the Good Life: Reason and the Passions in Greek, Cartesian and Psychoanalytic Ethics*. Cambridge: Cambridge University Press, 1998.

———. *Philosophy of Religion: Towards a More Humane Approach*. Cambridge: Cambridge University Press, 2014.

———. "The Question of Ageing." *Philosophical Papers* 41, no. 3 (2012): 371–96.

———. *The Rationalists*. Oxford: Oxford University Press, 1988.

Crane, Tim. "How We Can Be." *Times Literary Supplement*, 26 May 2017. https://www.the-tls.co.uk/articles/public/mind-body-problem-tim-crane/.

Dante Alighieri. *The Divine Comedy: Hell* [*La Divina Comedia: Inferno*; c. 1310]. Edited by G. Bickersteth. Oxford: Blackwell, 1981.

Darwin, Charles. *The Descent of Man and Selection in Relation to Sex* [1871]. London: Penguin, 2004.

Davidson, Donald. "Mental Events" [1970]. Essay 11 in *Essays on Actions and Events*. Oxford: Clarendon, 1980.

Davies, Brian. *Thomas Aquinas on God and Evil*. Oxford: Oxford University Press, 2011.

Day, Christopher. *Places of the Soul*. Abingdon: Routledge, 2014.

Defoe, Daniel. *An Essay upon Projects* [1697]. Project Gutenberg. https://www.gutenberg.org/ebooks/author/204.

Dennett, Daniel. *From Bacteria to Bach and Back*. New York: Norton, 2017.

———. "Who's On First? Heterophenomenology Explained." In "Trusting the Subject?" pt. 1, edited by Anthony I. Jack and Andreas Roepstorff, special issue, *Journal of Consciousness Studies* 10, no. 9 (October 2003): 19–30.

Descartes, René.
Note: The abbreviations 'AT', 'CSM' and 'CSMK', used in the footnotes for references to Descartes stand respectively for the works listed below as *Oeuvres de Descartes* and *The Philosophical Writings of Descartes*, Vols. 1 and 2, and Vol 3.
Conversation with Burman. Translated by J. Cottingham. Oxford: Clarendon, 1976.

———. *Discourse on the Method* [*Discours de la méthode*; 1637]. In AT, vol. 6, 1–78, and CSM, vol. 1, 110–51.

———. *Meditations on First Philosophy* [*Meditationes de prima philosophia*; 1641]. In AT, vol. 7, 17–90, and CSM, vol. 2, 12–62.

———. *Œuvres de Descartes*. Edited by C. Adam and P. Tannery. 12 vols. Revised ed. Paris: Vrin/CNRS, 1964–76. Cited as AT.

———. *The Philosophical Writings of Descartes*. Translated by J. Cottingham, R. Stoothoff, and D. Murdoch. Vols. 1 and 2. Cambridge: Cambridge University Press, 1985. Cited as CSM.

———. *The Philosophical Writings of Descartes*. Translated by J. Cottingham, R. Stoothoff, D. Murdoch, and A. Kenny. Vol. 3, *The Correspondence*. Cambridge: Cambridge University Press, 1991. Cited as CSMK.

———. *Principles of Philosophy* [*Principia philosophiae*; 1644]. In AT, vol. 8, 5–329, and CSM, vol. 1, 193–291.

———. *Rules for the Direction of the Mind* [*Regulae ad directionem ingenii; c.* 1628]. In AT, vol. 10, 359–472, and CSM, vol. 1, 9–78.

———. *Treatise on Man* [*Traité de l'homme; c.* 1633]. In AT, vol. 11, 120–202, and CSM, vol. 1, 99–108.

Dosick, Wayne. *Living Judaism*. New York: HarperCollins, 1995.

Dummett, Michael. *Thought and Reality*. Oxford: Clarendon, 2006.

Eddington, Arthur. *The Nature of The Physical World*. New York: Macmillan, 1928.

Eliot, George. *Silas Marner* [1861]. London: Penguin, 1996.

Eliot, T. S. *The Complete Poems and Plays*. New York: Harcourt Brace and World, 1961.

Ellis, Fiona. *God, Value, and Nature*. Oxford: Oxford University Press, 2015.

Empson, William. *Seven Types of Ambiguity* [1930]. Harmondsworth: Penguin, 1995.

Eustachius a Sancto Paulo. *Summa philosophiae quadripartita* [1609]. In *Descartes' Meditations: Background Source Materials*, translated and edited by R. Ariew, J. Cottingham, and T. Sorell, 68–96. Cambridge: Cambridge University Press, 1998.

Firestone, Chris, and Nathan Jacobs. *In Defense of Kant's Religion*. Bloomington: Indiana University Press, 2008.

Frege, Gottlob. *The Basic Laws of Arithmetic* [*Die Grundgesetze der Arithmetik*, vol. 1; 1893]. Translated by M. Furth. Berkeley: University of California Press, 1964.

Freud, Sigmund. *Civilization and Its Discontents* [*Das Unbehagen in der Kultur*; 1929]. In PFL, vol. 12, 251–340.

———. *Introductory Lectures on Psychoanalysis* [*Vorlesungen zur Einführung in die Psychoanalyse*; 1916–17]. In PFL, vol. 1, 39–518.

———. *New Lectures on Psychoanalysis* [*Neue Folge der Vorlesungen zur Einfürhung in die Psychoanalyse*; 1932]. In PFL, vol. 2, 8–226.

———. *The Penguin Freud Library*. Edited by James Strachey and Angela Richards. 15 vols. London: Penguin Books, 1985. Cited as PFL.

Freud, Sigmund, and J. Breuer. *Studies in Hysteria* [*Studien über Hysterie*; 1895]. In PFL, vol. 3, 53–335.

Gallup, G. "Self-Awareness in Primates." *American Scientist* 67 (1979): 417–21.

Gemes, Ken. "Postmodernism's Use and Abuse of Nietzsche." *Philosophy and Phenomenological Research* 62, no. 2 (2001): 337–60.

Geuss, Raymond. "Poetry and Knowledge." *Arion* 11, no. 1 (2003): 1–31.

Goetz, Stewart, and Charles Taliaferro. *A Brief History of the Soul*. Oxford: Wiley-Blackwell, 2007.

Goff, Philip. *Consciousness and Fundamental Reality*. Oxford: Oxford University Press, 2017.

Gregory, Brad. "No Room for God." *History and Theory* 47 (2008): 495–519.

Grice, Paul. "Method in Philosophical Psychology (From the Banal to the Bizarre)." *Proceedings and Addresses of the American Philosophical Association* 48 (1975): 23–53.

Haas, Ray. *Touching the Face of God: The Story of John Gillespie Magee*. Wilson, NC: High Flight Productions, 2014.

Hadot, Pierre. *Philosophy as a Way of Life* [*Exercises spirituels et philosophie antique*; 1987]. Oxford: Blackwell, 1955.

Hankinson, R. J. "Philosophy of Science." Ch. 4 in *The Cambridge Companion to Aristotle*, edited by J. Barnes. Cambridge: Cambridge University Press, 1995.

Hardy, Thomas. *Selected Poems*. Edited by R. Mezey. London: Penguin, 1998.

Harris, George. *Reason's Grief*. Cambridge: Cambridge University Press, 2006.

Hegel, Georg. *Phenomenology of Spirit* [*Phänomenologie des Geistes*; 1807]. Translated by A. V. Miller. Oxford: Clarendon, 1997.

Hopkins, Gerard Manley. *Poems and Prose*. Edited by W. H. Gardner. Harmondsworth: Penguin, 1953.

Housman, A. E. *Last Poems* [1922]. In *Collected Poems*, 105–55. Harmondsworth: Penguin, 1956.

Hume, David. *An Enquiry concerning Human Understanding* [1748]. Edited by T. Beauchamp. Oxford: Oxford University Press, 1999.

Humphrey, Nicholas. *Soul Dust*. London: Quercus, 2012.

Insole, Christopher. *The Intolerable God: Kant's Theological Journey*. Grand Rapids, MI: Eerdmans, 2016.

James, William. *Pragmatism* [1907]. In *Pragmatism and Other Writings*, 1–132. London: Penguin, 2000.

———. *Principles of Psychology* [1890]. Vol. 1. Cambridge, MA: Harvard University Press, 1981.

Jaworski, William. *Structure and the Metaphysics of Mind: How Hylomorphism Solves the Mind-Body Problem*. Oxford: Oxford University Press, 2016.

Johnston, Mark. *Saving God: Religion after Idolatry*. Princeton, NJ: Princeton University Press, 2009.

Jung, Carl. *Aion* [1951]. Pt. 2 of CW, vol. 9.

———. *Collected Works*. Translated by G. Adler and R.F.C. Hull. Rev. ed. 20 vols. London: Routledge, 1967–77. Cited as CW.

———. "Problems of Modern Psychotherapy" [*Die Probleme der modernen Psychotherapie*; 1929]. Translated by Cary Baynes. In *Modern Man in Search of a Soul*, 32–62. London: Routledge, 1993.

————. *Psychology and Religion* [first published in English 1938]. In CW, vol. 11, 89–95.

————. *Symbols of Transformation* [*Wandlungen und Symbole der Libido*; 1912]. Vol. 5 of CW.

Kahneman, David. *Thinking Fast and Slow*. London: Penguin, 2011.

Kant, Immanuel. *Critique of Practical Reason* [*Kritik der Practischen Vernunft*; 1788]. Translated by T. K. Abbott. 6th ed. London: Longmans, 1909.

————. *Critique of Pure Reason* [*Kritik der Reinen Vernunft*; 1st ed. ("A") 1781; 2nd ed. ("B") 1787]. Translated by N. Kemp Smith. New York: Macmillan, 1929.

————. *Groundwork of the Metaphysic of Morals* [*Grundlegung zur Metaphysik der Sitten*; 1785]. Vol. 4 of the Akademie edition. Berlin: Reimer/de Gruyter, 1900–. Translated by T. E. Hill Jr. and A. Zweig. Oxford: Oxford University Press, 2003.

————. *Metaphysic of Morals* [*Metaphysik der Sitten*; 1797]. Edited by M. Gregor. Cambridge: Cambridge University Press, 1996.

————. *Opus postumum*. In Vols. 21 and 22, of the Akademie edition. Berlin: de Gruyter, 1936. Translated by E. Förster and M. Rosen. Cambridge: Cambridge University Press, 1993.

Kass, Leon. *The Hungry Soul: Eating and the Perfecting of our Nature*. New York: Macmillan, 1994.

Kierkegaard, Søren. *Sickness unto Death* [*Sygdommen til Døden*; 1849]. Edited by H. and E. Hong. Princeton, NJ: Princeton University Press, 1980.

Kihlstrom, John. "The Cognitive Unconscious." *Science* 237 (1987): 1445–52.

Kipling, Rudyard. *Kim* [1901]. Ware: Wordsworth, 1993.

Kirk, Robert. "Zombies." *Stanford Encyclopedia of Philosophy*. Edited by Edward N. Zalta. Summer 2015 edition. First published 8 September 2003; substantive revision 16 March 2015, last revised summer 2015. http://plato.stanford.edu/entries /zombies/.

Korsgaard, Christine. *Self-Constitution: Agency, Identity, and Integrity*. Oxford: Oxford University Press, 2009.

————. *The Sources of Normativity*. Cambridge: Cambridge University Press, 1996.

Lacan, Jacques. *The Four Fundamental Concepts of Psychoanalysis* [1973]. Translated by A. Sheridan. Harmondsworth: Penguin, 1979.

Lear, Jonathan. *Wisdom Won from Illness*. Cambridge, MA: Harvard University Press, 2017.

Leibniz, Gottfried. *Monadology* [*La monadologie*; 1714]. Translated in *Philosophical Writings*, edited by G.H.R. Parkinson, 179–94. London: Dent, 1973.

Levinas, Emmanuel. "Beyond Intentionality." In *Philosophy in France Today*, edited by Alan Montefiore, 100–115. Cambridge: Cambridge University Press, 1983.

————. *Totality and Infinity* [*Totalité et infini*; 1961]. Translated by A. Lingis. Dordrecht: Kluwer, 1991.

Locke, John. *An Essay concerning Human Understanding* [1690]. Oxford: Clarendon, 1975.

Long, A., and D. N. Sedley, eds. *The Hellenistic Philosophers*. Cambridge: Cambridge University Press, 1987.

MacIntyre, Alasdair. *Ethics in the Conflicts of Modernity: An Essay on Desire, Practical Reasoning, and Narrative*. Cambridge: Cambridge University Press, 2016.

Malebranche, Nicolas. *Méditations chrétiennes et métaphysiques* [1683]. Paris: Vrin, 1896.

————. *The Search after Truth* [*La recherche de la vérité*; 6th ed., 1712]. Translated by T. Lennon and P. Olscamp. Cambridge: Cambridge University Press, 1997.

Marlowe, Christopher. *The Tragical History of the Life and Death of Doctor Faustus* [*c.* 1690]. Harlow: Pearson, 2003.

May, Simon. *Love: A History*. New Haven, CT: Yale University Press, 2014.

McGilchrist, Iain. *The Master and His Emissary*. New Haven, CT: Yale University Press, 2009.

McGinn, Colin. *The Mysterious Flame: Conscious Minds in a Material World*. New York: Basic Books, 1999.

McPherson, David. "Cosmic Outlooks and Neo-Aristotelian Virtue Ethics." *International Philosophical Quarterly* 55, no. 2 (2015): 197–215.

Melamed, Yitzhak. "Cohen, Spinoza and the Nature of Pantheism." *Jewish Studies Quarterly* 25 (2018): 1–10.

Moltmann, Jürgen. *God in Creation*. London: SCM, 1985.

Moser, Paul. *The Elusive God: Reorienting Religious Epistemology*. Cambridge: Cambridge University Press, 2008.

————. *The Evidence for God*. Cambridge: Cambridge University Press, 2010.

Mulgan, Tim. *Purpose in the Universe*. Oxford: Oxford University Press, 2015.

Murdoch, Iris. *Metaphysics as a Guide to Morals*. London: Penguin, 1992.

Nagel, Thomas. *Mind and Cosmos*. Oxford: Oxford University Press, 2012.

————. *Mortal Questions*. Cambridge: Cambridge University Press, 1979.

————. *Secular Philosophy and the Religious Temperament*. Oxford: Oxford University Press, 2010.

————. *The View from Nowhere*. New York: Oxford University Press, 1986.

————. "What Is It Like to Be a Bat?" [1974]. Ch. 12 in *Mortal Questions*.

Nehamas, Alexander. *The Art of Living: Socratic Reflections from Plato to Foucault*. Berkeley: University of California Press, 1998.

Nietzsche, Friedrich. *Beyond Good and Evil* [*Jenseits von Gut und Böse*; 1886]. Translated by W. Kaufmann. New York: Random House, 1966.

————. *Thus Spake Zarathustra* [*Also Sprach Zarathustra*; 1883–91]. London: Penguin, 1969.

————. *Twilight of the Idols* [*Götzen-dämmerung*; 1889]. Translated by R. Hollingdale. London: Penguin, 1990.

————. *Untimely Meditations* [*Unzeitmässe Betrachtungen*; 1876]. Cambridge: Cambridge University Press, 1997.

O'Neil, Onora. *Constructions of Reason*. Cambridge: Cambridge University Press, 1989.

Palmer, Michael. *Freud and Jung on Religion*. London: Routledge, 1977.

Papineau, David. "Papineau vs Dennett: A Philosophical Dispute." *Times Literary Supplement*. 2 August 2017. https://www.the-tls.co.uk/articles/public/dennett -papineau-debate.

Parfit, Derek. *On What Matters*. Oxford: Oxford University Press, 2011.

Plato. *Apology* [*c*. 390 BCE]. Translated by Hugh Tredennick. Harmondsworth: Penguin, 1956.

————. *Meno* [*c*. 380 BCE]. Translated by W.C.K. Guthrie. Harmondsworth: Penguin, 1956.

————. *Phaedo* [*c*. 390 BCE]. Translated by Hugh Tredennick. London: Penguin, 2005.

————. *Republic* [*c*. 375 BCE]. Translated by Desmond Lee. London: Penguin, 2007.

Priest, Stephen. "Radical Internalism." *Journal of Consciousness Studies* 13 (2006): 147–74.

Pullman, Philip. *Northern Lights*. London: Scholastic, 1995.

Radcliffe, Timothy. *Why Go to Church: The Drama of the Eucharist*. London: Continuum, 2008.

Rahner, Karl. *Foundations of Christian Faith* [*Grundkurs des Glaubens*; 1976]. London: Darton, Longman and Todd, 1978.

Rilke, Rainer Maria. *Neue gedichte/New Poems*. Translated by S. Cohn. Manchester: Carcanet, 1997.

Rosenzweig, Franz. *The Star of Redemption* [*Der Stern der Erlösung*; 1921]. Heidelberg: Lambert Schneider, 1954.

Russell, Bertrand. *The Analysis of Matter* [1927]. London: Routledge, 1992.

————. *Problems of Philosophy* [1912]. Oxford: Oxford University Press, 1967.

Ryle, Gilbert. *The Concept of Mind*. London: Hutcheson, 1949.

Scruton, Roger. *Human Nature*. Princeton, NJ: Princeton University Press, 2017.

Sellars, Wilfred. *Empiricism and the Philosophy of Mind* [1956]. Cambridge, MA: Harvard University Press, 1997.

Seneca. *Epistulae morales* [64 CE]. Oxford: Oxford University Press, 1967.

Shafer-Landau, Russ, ed. *Ethical Theory*. Oxford: Blackwell, 2013.

————. *Moral Realism*. Oxford: Clarendon, 2003.

Shakespeare, William. *Complete Works*. Edited by C. J. Sisson. London: Odhams, 1953.

Spinoza, Benedict. *Ethics* [*Ethica ordine geometrico demonstrata; c. 1665*]. Translated by E. Curley. Princeton, NJ: Princeton University Press, 1985.

Strawson, Galen. "Against Narrativity." In *The Self*, edited by Strawson, 63–86. Oxford: Blackwell, 2005.

Suarez, Francisco. *Metaphysical Disputations* [*Disputationes metaphysicae; 1597*]. Vol. 26 of *Opera Omnia*, edited by C. Berton. Paris: Vives, 1856.

Swinburne, Richard. *The Evolution of the Soul*. Oxford: Clarendon, 2005.

Taylor, Charles. *A Secular Age*. Cambridge, MA: Harvard University Press, 2007.

————. *Sources of the Self*. Cambridge: Cambridge University Press, 1989.

Tyler, Peter. *The Pursuit of the Soul*. London: Bloomsbury, 2016.

Voss, Stephen. "The End of Anthropology." In *Reason, Will and Sensation*, edited by J. Cottingham, 273–306. Oxford: Oxford University Press, 1994.

Ward, Graham. *Unbelievable: Why We Believe and Why We Don't*. London: Tauris, 2014.

Weber, Max. "Science as a Profession" [*Wissenschaft als Beruf; 1920*]. Translated in *Max Weber: Essays in Sociology*, edited by H. H. Gerth and C. Wright Mills, 129–56. New York: Oxford University Press, 1946.

White, Victor. *God and the Unconscious* [1952]. London: Collins, 1960.

Wielenberg, Eric. *Value and Virtue in a Godless Universe*. Cambridge: Cambridge University Press, 2005.

Williams, Bernard. *Ethics and the Limits of Philosophy*. London: Collins/Fontana, 1985.

————. *Making Sense of Humanity*. Cambridge: Cambridge University Press, 1995.

————. "Moral Luck" [1976]. In *Moral Luck: Philosophical Papers 1973–1980*, 20–39. Cambridge: Cambridge University Press, 1981.

Wittgenstein, Ludwig. *Philosophical Investigations* [*Philosophische Untersuchungen*; 1953]. Translated by G.E.M. Anscombe. New York: Macmillan, 1958.

Wordsworth, William. *A Critical Edition of the Major Works*. Edited by S. Gill. Oxford: Oxford University Press, 2010.

————. "Lines Composed a Few Miles above Tintern Abbey" [1798]. In *Critical Edition*, 131–35.

Yeats, William Butler. *Collected Poems*. London: Macmillan, 1963.

INDEX

truth: inner human being, dwelling within, 101–3; moral, 85–87 (*see also* morality; normativity); problems in the quest for, 103–6; science as the measure of all, 26, 74, 82 (*see also* science); the world presented to consciousness as, 95, 99 (*see also* reality)

Ward, Graham, 112–13
Weber, Max, 10

White, Victor, 114
Wielenberg, Eric, 86
Williams, Bernard, 15, 153
Wittgenstein, Ludwig, 31, 42, 75
Wordsworth, William, 11–13, 94, 140–41, 152, 156
worship, 148

Yeats, William Butler, 64–65